GEORGE SMITH
The Children's Friend

George Smith of Coalville aged 40

"It is the children! The cause of the children! The education and protection of the children! I want to the front."

George Smith to the editor of *The Graphic* who insisted on Smith's portrait appearing in an article about his work.

GEORGE SMITH

The Children's Friend

Adrian Bristow

IMOGEN

George Smith   The Children's Friend
First published in England by
Imogen
1 Greenacre Road
CHESTER
CH4 7NH

© 1999 Adrian Bristow

All Rights Reserved.
No part of this publication may be reproduced,
stored in a retrieval system, or transmitted
in any form or by any means, electronic,
mechanical, photocopying, recording or
otherwise, without the prior permission
of the Copyright holder.

To My Daughters
Alison, Rosalind and Philippa

ISBN 0-9535002-0-9

A CIP catalogue entry for this book
is available from the British Library

Printed and bound by
Bridge Books, Wrexham

Contents

	Preface	7
Chapter 1:	Arrival at Clayhills	9
Chapter 2:	Early Stirrings	17
Chapter 3:	Prelude to Coalville	29
Chapter 4:	Drama and Dissention	37
Chapter 5:	The Dream	51
Chapter 6:	The Dream Realised	59
Chapter 7:	Little Local Difficulties	71
Chapter 8:	The Political Animal	80
Chapter 9:	Death, Dismissal and a Dismal Departure	86
Chapter 10:	The Canal Campaign: Opening Salvos	94
Chapter 11:	Winning Ways and Winter Walks	105
Chapter 12:	An Inland Voyage	115
Chapter 13:	Bread and Circuses	130
Chapter 14:	The Romany Rye	145
Chapter 15:	A Band of Brothers	154
Chapter 16:	Journey's End	166
	Books by George Smith	177
	Select Bibliography	178
	Index	179

Illustrations

George Smith of Coalville aged 40	*Frontispiece*
A Dame School	18
Children at the Pug Mill	21
A brick-yard child	23
An exhausted oven girl	24
Children counting their wages	26
Coalville Primitive Methodist Chapel and Schoolroom	43
The Earl of Shaftesbury	61
Narrow boats on the Regent Canal in 1823	95
Plan of a narrow boat cabin	97
Cabin interior from the bed	98
Cabin interior from the door	101
The Animals	104
Dedication to *Canal Adventures by Moonlight*	111
The Canal Boatmen's Magazine	113
South View, 14 Ashby Road, Welton, Northants.	120
Queen's House, Crick, formerly The Cabin	129
George Smith in Notting Dale, London (1879)	132
Gypsy quarters, Plaistow Marshes	133
Encampment at Mitcham Common	134
'The Little Azella'	137
A young acrobat: Lulu	138
Little Nell at Mrs. Jarley's Waxworks	139
Jerry and his dancing dogs	140
George Smith visiting gypsy children near London	142
White Cottage and Queen's House	157
George Smith aged 63	169

Preface

The only previous biography of George Smith was published in 1896, the year after his death. It was written by Edward Hodder, who had already produced a three-volume biography of that doyen of Victorian reformers, Lord Shaftesbury, and was thus admirably qualified to deal with a minor and a more humble figure. Although Hodder had not known Smith personally, he was aware of his work on behalf of the children. He met Mary Smith and members of her family and he sought out people in various walks of life who had known Smith and whose appearance, character, behaviour and achievements were still fresh in their minds. Thus Hodder's biography is our major source for material about Smith's life and work.

There are, however, other sources. Some snippets of personal information are contained in articles and letters written by Smith which he included in certain of his books. Again, a few years before his death, Smith wrote a curious autobiographical booklet of some forty-eight pages called *An Open Letter to my Friends; or Sorrows and Joys at Bosvil* [Coalville]. He had it printed for private circulation in 1892 and it was widely distributed among his friends and supporters. Although published thirty years after the unfortunate events in his business career in Coalville it describes, *An Open Letter* is a valuable source document because it also contains brief accounts of his political activities in Coalville during the period 1867–1874 and his work there for the Sunday School movement.

Finally, there are the diaries. In 1876 Smith began to keep a diary and he continued to do this until he died in 1895. It was a daily record of what he did, the people he met, the things he heard or said, his hopes and fears, his expenditure and details of his vivid dreams. After his death these voluminous diaries were carefully kept by his eldest son, Dr. Grosart Smith, a general practitioner, who continued to live at Smith's old home, The Cabin, in Crick, later re-christened Queen's House. He stored them away in the attic along with unsold copies of Smith's books and pamphlets. When Dr. Smith died in 1952, his two daughters, Valerie and Mary, had the task of sorting out his effects. They came across a dusty pile of their grandfather's diaries and, not realising their value, burned them.

This was unfortunate for later biographers. At least Hodder had access to the diaries for his biography; he quotes a number of the entries in his book but he did not make as extensive use of the diaries as one might have expected. In fact, he confessed that they were wearisome reading and rather left it at that. Hodder did concede that they illustrated facets of Smith's character, provided evidence of the sheer volume of work he accomplished and the amount of travelling and lobbying he undertook.

Besides the diaries, Smith also kept what I suppose is a cross between a correspondence book and a cuttings book. I have examined this book, a very large one indeed, with black covers and a heavy brass clasp. In it Smith kept copies of his letters to Queen Victoria and brief acknowledgements by her private secretary of the letters, articles and books Smith so sedulously sent her. It also contained a number of press cuttings but these proved of little value since they duplicated material contained in his books.

Today George Smith and his work on behalf of the exploited and brutalised children in the second half of the nineteenth century are virtually forgotten. If Smith is mentioned at all, it is in books about canals — and then briefly — where he is usually described as an active and enthusiastic reformer known as the "Children's Friend". The only critical appreciation of any aspect of his work is that contained in the chapter headed, 'Our Canal Population' in Harry Hanson's book, *The Canal Boatmen: 1760–1914*, which deals with his work on behalf of the canal children. This chapter challenges a number of unsupported statements made by Smith in various publications during his canal campaign. Though Hanson is broadly appreciative of Smith's efforts, he successfully refutes several of his wilder assertions.

Smith's memory, alas, has not been kept green. While Lord Shaftesbury towers above the other reformers of the Victorian age, the name of Smith wakes few echoes down the passages of time. This book is an attempt to ensure that the struggles and achievements of this enthusiastic, vain, stout-hearted, stubborn, humble, deeply religious and combative reformer should be remembered, and that his contribution to the welfare of thousands of unfortunate children should be recognised.

Adrian Bristow
Chester, 1998

Chapter 1: Arrival at Clayhills

"The Egyptians made the Children of Israel to serve with rigour: and they made their lives bitter with hard bondage, in mortar, and in brick, and in all manner of service in the field."

Exodus I 13, 14

This is the story of the life and achievements of an obscure Victorian reformer and philanthropist called George Smith. He was a man from the poorest of backgrounds who devoted his life to improving the conditions of children working in the brutalising atmosphere of brick-yards and canal boats. He also attempted to improve the lot of 'travelling' children, as they were known, including gypsy children and the children of van dwellers working in fairs and circuses.

Although the memory of many outstanding social reformers such as Shaftesbury, Sadler, Plimsoll and Oastler, the 'Factory King', is still fresh today, the name of George Smith and his work to end the abuses of child-labour have slipped into oblivion. It might be claimed for this complex man, active Methodist, successful businessman, indefatigable in his pursuit of reform, that he tried with much success to end the worst excesses of child-labour in areas of industry untouched by Shaftesbury's far-reaching reforms. It is a particularly pleasing and worthwhile task to write the life of a man whose love and concern for children was the mainspring of his existence and to try to resurrect a deserved reputation of over a century ago.

For a biographer to be saddled at the outset with a subject called by the most common of surnames is rather embarrassing, especially when this is prefixed by the simple Christian name, George. There is little magic here. However, he can console himself with the thought that there have been a number of famous Smiths, ranging from Adam, Sydney and F.E. to John, rescued by Pocahontas, and Joseph, founder of the Mormons. In the *Dictionary of National Biography* there are several pages of minor and major Smiths. By a happy coincidence it was another George Smith, publisher of many of the Victorian novelists and poets, who was the founder and proprietor of it.

Yet, in a way, his name is most apt: straight-forward, blunt and uncompromising like the man. I did not add 'modest' because Smith in later life had developed a proper regard for his abilities and experience. There was in him a streak of vanity and a vein of pride, though perhaps both these blemishes can be forgiven in view of his achievements. Certainly he was modest about his lack of education but this did not stop him from becoming an effective speaker, a prosperous manager and a writer, on occasions, of great sincerity and emotional power. Springing from humble stock, he recommended Christian humility to others and lay claim to a staggering amount of it himself, but he was humble only before his God. His essential goodness made him a Pickwick and not a Uriah Heap.

Smith, revealingly, was rather proud of his surname, and he took considerable trouble to discover whether he was perhaps a Smith of a very high order indeed. He speculated:

> It is more than probable that we are the descendants of William Smith Stanley the second, or William Smith Stanley the third, or Adam Smith Stanley, the son of Sir William Smith Stanley, the fourth Lord of Stanley.

These were but idle dreams; but Smith was much given to dreams and their interpretation, as we shall see.

An American friend of his, also called Smith, who knew of his pre-occupation, sent him the following verses:

> Of all the ancient families
> That dwell upon the earth,
> The most unique, if not antique,
> Is that which gave us birth.
>
> For on Egyptian obelisk,
> And Grecian monolith,
> You'll find enrolled, in letters bold,
> The honoured name of Smith.
>
> From Arctic seas to tropic lands
> We've lots of kin and kith,
> No list elite is quite complete
> Without the name of Smith.

One can only conjecture what Smith, who sadly lacked a sense of humour, made of this.

George Smith was the son of William Smith, an unknown and

impoverished worker in the brick-yards of the Potteries. It is rare for anything to be known about the obscure father of an obscure reformer whose achievements have long been forgotten. But we are lucky in William's case for, thanks to a curious 'brief life' (it can hardly be called a biography), we know a little about the unremarkable life of this unremarkable man. Since the influence of George Smith's parents and home shaped his religious beliefs and attitudes, it is fortunate that we can look at his father's life in some detail.

After William's death in 1872, George was determined to celebrate his father's memory with a biography. Soon afterwards, while on one of his many visits to London during his campaign on behalf of canal boat children, he chanced to meet the Rev. Alexander Balloch Grosart, the Scottish Presbyterian Minister of St. George's, Blackburn. Grosart is yet another of those many Victorians who still have the power to astonish us by their industry. Licensed by Edinburgh Presbytery in 1856, he worked first at Kinross and then at Prince's Park, Liverpool, before finally dropping anchor as minister of St. George's, Blackburn. Here he made his name as an editor of reprints of rare items of Elizabethan and Jacobean literature. He also edited the works of several Puritan divines and, in between, found time to publish several original devotional works. He ministered at Blackburn from 1868 to 1872 and in this period alone he edited more than 130 volumes! Perhaps his pastoral duties were not unduly pressing, although there is no reason to believe he did not fling himself into these as enthusiastically as he did into literature. This chance encounter in London proved to be a meeting of like minds and Smith asked Grosart to write a memoir of his father's life. Presumably he suggested a memoir because he felt there was hardly enough material to justify a biography. Grosart made some excuse (his life was not exactly empty), but when Smith pressed him again, and Smith was nothing if not tenacious, he apparently felt unable to refuse. The book was finally published in 1874 under the title *Hanani or Memoir of William Smith*. It was Grosart's idea to give George Smith's father the sobriquet of Hanani; it is a reference to Nehemiah VII 2: "My brother Hanani.... He was a faithful man and feared God above many."

In the introductory letter printed with it, Grosart confirms that he was asked more than once by George Smith (whom he compares in 'noble indiscretions' with that other reformer of the period, Samuel Plimsoll) to write about his father, who later became a Primitive Methodist Local Preacher. He adds: "I make no claim for your father of greatness or such kind of remarkableness as marks men out from their fellows, intellectually and otherwise. But I do claim for him goodness of a very real and Christlike type — such goodness as I think has a very much needed message for many in pulpit and pew alike".

Smith supplied the reluctant author with certain notebooks his father kept and these, plus whatever Smith told him of his own recollections of his father's life, provided the scanty basis for what turned out to be a somewhat perfunctory memoir. Most of what little factual information it contains deals with William Smith's parents and their home near Chesterton, a small village a few miles from Stoke-on-Trent. Grosart quotes long extracts from George Smith's later book about his experiences in the brick-fields, *The Cry of the Children*, and includes lengthy passages of drivel from his father's notebooks. But by this time loyalty to his subject was wearing rather thin and Grosart admitted the notebooks were ill-spelt and poorly written. To this farrago, Grosart added his own lengthy philosophising of a rhapsodic kind — or you might say his lengthy rhapsodising of a philosophic kind. With Grosart's prose style (or with George Smith's at emotional moments) it doesn't really matter, matter, matter, matter, matter, matter.

It is sad that this rambling memoir tells us nothing of William Smith's adult life for the thirty years from 1832–1862. It says nothing of his four children and throws no light whatsoever upon his relations with his eldest son George. There is a steel engraving in the book of the adult William, a figure who bears a strong resemblance to later portraits of his son. There is the same high round balding dome, and beneath it a rubicund bespectacled face, heavily whiskered in the fashion of the age. A fierce Old Testament benevolence blazes out.

Grosart relates how William Smith was the eldest of the ten children of John and Deborah Smith (née Capper). He was born at Chesterton on 8th February, 1807 in one of three workman's cottages which had been made out of a large dilapidated farmhouse that bore the imposing name of 'Canal Hall'. In fact, 'canal' was a corruption of 'cannel', a type of hard coal found locally and of which the 'Hall' was actually built. This is not as fanciful as it seems. Cannel could be cut and polished into ornaments such as candlesticks and snuff boxes. It was so clean it was claimed that a summer house made of it at Haigh Hall near Wigan never soiled the ladies' dresses. His mother, with little money to keep an increasing family, proved to be a woman of sterling worth. Grosart records that "she was village-doctor, village-nurse, village-missionary and village-every thing when kindly, undemonstrative help was needed." Even forty years later, so it was said, anyone connected with "good old Deborah Smith" was guaranteed a warm welcome in the cottages in the Chesterton district.

Both his parents worked in the local brick-yard and at the age of five William joined his father there. This meant a walk of two and a half miles to the brick-yard in time for a six o'clock start. His normal working day lasted fourteen hours in the summer but considerably less during the winter. He spent long hours carrying clay on his head to the moulding sheds and later carrying finished bricks to the kiln. This was the pattern of his employment until he was fourteen when he was promoted to the job of wheeling clay from the pits. He worked four years at this barrowing, spending the last four hours of the day in winter in the moulding sheds, when it became too dark to see where he was going.

He received little education, acquiring only the rudiments of the three Rs at a Sunday School, and he never sought to fill the gaps in his education in later life. William seems to have accepted his lot in life as natural and unavoidable and he admitted to George later on that he was very slow to realise the monstrousness of child labour. Certainly he never blamed his father for putting him to work in the brick-yard.

In the industrial areas of Staffordshire in the nineteenth century nearly all poor boys found themselves employed in the mines, mills or brick-yards from an early age. This was the general fate and one from which few managed to escape. William was one of the few. As he matured, he developed into an able craftsman. He had the ability and the force of character to rise above an environment that crushed the spirit and humanity out of hundreds of thousands of his fellows. In his early twenties, on his journeys to and from the brick-yard, he met and fell in love with a young woman called Hannah Hollins, two years older than himself and a worker in a local pottery. In March, 1830 they were married at Wolstanton Parish Church. It was about the time of his marriage that William became converted. This was not achieved, so we are told, without an inward struggle that raged at home and at work for some three months. Finally, when he was praying on his knees by the brick table (which must have taken some moral courage), "he seemed actually to see his Divine Saviour" and thenceforth became a man of God. His conversion filled him with a peace, a joy, and a hope that never left him.

At this time in his life William was a quick-tempered, impetuous and passionate man, qualities he was to pass on to his son, but he slowly mellowed after his conversion and marriage. Always honest and upright, he now he became a God-fearing man of a simple and rigorous piety with a strong evangelical streak. He became an active member of the local Primitive Methodist Chapel and started preaching, tentatively at first but with growing confidence as he tried to convey the joy and satisfaction that the love of God had brought him. William's religion became a very personal one and as he grew older, he developed a feeling of direct communication with God. Writing in his note-book William uses some unusual workaday imagery:

> Whilst at prayer my mind was rather shifting. I had to bring it back and ask it to sit down.
> It did so. The Lord helped me.
> Deep solemn sense of God's presence this morning; [determined] to enlighten my mind, to read and mind my stops better, to give the sense in reading, that I may be more useful to myself and others.
> When I ask anything of God, may I ask properly, becomingly with good manners. My mind was something like a horse when his shoulders are stiff; would not go to work at all; he wants tapping on the neck a bit.

This habit rubbed off on his son. For example, we find George writing in his diary for 25th November 1870: "I was as close to the Lord as the coat upon my back."

Prayer now played a vital part in William's life. He had stated times for prayer; twice a day for family worship and three times a day for private prayer. This latter he pursued with zest, no matter where he found himself, whether he was walking along the road, working at the brick table or at the kiln. He once wrote, "It were as rational to expect a fire to burn without fuel as a Christian to live without private devotion."

Some months after their marriage William and Hannah left Chesterton and set up home in Clayhills, a part of Tunstall, the most northerly of the towns and villages that formed the area known as the Potteries. As its name suggests, Clayhills was one of the many places in the region where large beds of clay could be easily worked. In 1830 Clayhills consisted of a few cottages and houses on the west side of Tunstall where the ground fell away from the road towards Brindley's Trent and Mersey Canal. The Potteries had been one of the first regions in England to experience explosive growth under the impact of the industrial revolution. North Staffordshire had been a pottery centre since 1700 thanks to its easily accessible deposits of various types of clay. And, later, when supplying wood for the kilns became a problem, coal was found in abundance in the district. Yet for what was essentially a small scale industry to develop further, an improved means of transport was necessary. The catalyst appeared in the guise of a canal. The canal network in the North-West and Midlands was still in its infancy but, through the efforts of the energetic and far-sighted Josiah Wedgwood, the Trent and Mersey Canal was opened in 1777. This revolution in transport opened up the whole of North Staffordshire to industrial development, and brick-yards, potteries, collieries and iron works expanded and flourished. Transport costs fell dramatically and by the turn of the century Stoke-on-Trent had become the major centre in the country for pottery and a thriving producer of bricks, tiles, pipes and sanitary ware. The industrial revolution wreaked havoc on the landscape of the Potteries brick-fields, potbanks and collieries created a torn and derelict land criss-crossed by railway lines and canals. During the nineteenth century the Potteries became a dismal region dotted with bottle-shaped kilns belching smoke and punctuated by pithead winding gear, slag heaps and clay workings.

Today there are still traces of attractive countryside on the Clayhills side of Tunstall but it is a dreary prospect even on a warm summer day. To this ravaged landscape has been added an ironworks, a sewage plant and a motorway link. It is not a lovely sight. Clayhills itself no longer appears in the Ordnance Survey map; it has been obliterated. The only evidence of it is a small group of council houses called Clayhills built on rising ground by the cemetery. All the old cottages the Smiths knew have long since been swept away and redevelopment proceeds apace. Nothing remains on this desolate hillside of the Wesleyan and Primitive Methodist Chapels and their Sunday Schools round which so much of the religious, social and educational life of this small community once revolved.

It is difficult to over-estimate the role and significance of the non-conformist chapels at this period in the new manufacturing towns and villages of the North and Midlands. Here the presence of the Church of England was conspicuous by its absence; in any case there was little place and less function for the poor within its echoing gloom. But the Methodist Chapels sprang up everywhere, keeping pace with the growth of the new communities. Within their plain walls the labouring classes drew comfort from an emotional atmosphere heightened by music and singing all of which added a little colour and excitement to their drab existence.

William and Hannah soon established themselves in Clayhills. William found work in a local brick-yard, Peake's Tileries, one of several yards controlled by Thomas Peake and known as the Tunstall Tileries. He and Hannah lived about a hundred yards from the canal in a small cottage (owned by Peake) for which they paid the sum of £4.10s.0 per year. They were quite close to the recently-completed Harecastle Tunnel. When this was built so great was the demand for bricks for canal and railway engineering that the existing brick-yards could not supply the vast quantity of bricks needed for it. As a result, temporary works on the site were set up between 1822 and 1827 and these produced over seven million new bricks for the tunnel. The young couple joined the Wesleyan Chapel in America Street in Tunstall, and became devout and regular attenders. Both had good singing voices, especially Hannah, who became and remained a pillar of the choir for some nine years. It was here in the close-knit community of Clayhills that Hannah gave birth to their first child, George, on 16th February, 1831.

Chapter 2: Early Stirrings

> "The old-men, monkey-like faces, the shrunken, shivering, cowering, scared looks of many of the children are things not to be imagined. I hesitate not to say that the 'Society for the Protection of Lower Animals' would not allow a tithe of the cruelty perpetuated upon the brick-yard children to be done to the over-worked horse, donkey and the like."
>
> George Smith: *The Cry of the Children*

When he was four years old, George was enrolled by his parents in the Sunday School of their chapel. Besides its obvious function, a Sunday School provided a valuable educational function for hundreds of thousands of poor children before the coming of compulsory primary education. They were started in 1780 under the enthusiastic promotion of Robert Raikes and it is sometimes forgotten that the Sunday School movement was, with the Charity Schools, the pioneer of popular elementary education. In these early Wesleyan Methodist Sunday Schools, reading and writing were taught as a necessary preparation for the study of the Bible. Strongly encouraged by John Wesley himself, they proved most successful and by 1884 they contained more than a third of a million children and 60,000 teachers. If there was an emphasis on training the children of the poor to be industrious and amenable members of a sharply defined social order, this was no more than a reflection of the late eighteenth century and early nineteenth century views on class distinction and the need for due subordination from the lower orders. About this time George also started attending a Dame School in Clayhills run by Mrs. Betty Wedgwood, a Primitive Methodist and something of a character.

We tend to speak disparagingly of Dame Schools, which were provided by the working-class for working-class children, and to dismiss their importance. Yet they were found throughout the country and provide an example of the aspirations of the poor. As Shenstone wrote:

> In every village marked with little spire,
> Embower'd in trees and hardly known to fame,
> There dwells, in lowly shed and mean attire,

> A matron whom we schoolmistress name,
> Who boasts unruly brats with birch to tame.

They attracted popular support by their informality and their similarity to the homes from which the pupils came. Parents appreciated what were, in effect, their own schools and they continued to send their children to them despite the authorities deploring the lack of training among the teachers.

Few pictures of what life was like for the unruly brats in a small Dame School in the 1830s have come down to us but again we are fortunate in George Smith's case. A boy called Charles Shaw attended Mrs. Wedgwood's school with George and wrote a series of vivid reminiscences entitled, *When I was a Child; or, Some Phases of Social Life Fifty years ago by an Old Pottery Lad* for a Staffordshire newspaper. Shaw wrote:

> Dame Betty Wedgwood's school was in the only room on the ground floor of her little cottage. It was about four yards square, with a winding narrow staircase leading to the one bedroom above. The furniture was very scant, consisting of a small table, two chairs, and two or three little forms about eight inches high for the children to sit upon. There were a few pictures on the walls, of the usual garish sort, blazing with colour, and all the figures upon them in strikingly dramatic attitudes.
>
> The course of education given by the old lady was very simple, and graded with almost scientific precision. There was an alphabet with rude

A Dame School

pictures for beginners. I have an impression, too, that the distinctness of that old alphabet had something to do with the success of Old Betty's teaching, for, though she never taught writing, her scholars were generally noted for their ability to read while very young.

Betty's next grade after the alphabet was the reading-made-easy book, with black letters, making words in two, three and four letters. The next stage was spelling and reading of the Bible. For those successful in these higher stages, Old Betty had peculiar honours. They were allowed to take the ashes from under the fire-grate to the ashheap outside the house. This ash-heap was a common meeting place as everyone used it, and on its elevation many doughty battles were fought. There was yet another distinction the old lady had to bestow. She taught both girls and boys who were successful in reading how to knit stockings. I knew boys who knitted stockings for their family. They thus learnt reading and knitting instead of reading and writing.

The end of this idyll was fast approaching for young George. In 1838 he was removed from the Dame School and at the age of seven put to work making bricks alongside a relative at Peake's Tileries. George does not name this relative. He simply observes that "like most of his clan at that time, and like many now, he thought that kicks and blows were the best means of obtaining the maximum work from a lad". Despite his own unhappy experiences in the brick-fields, his father seems to have had little compunction in condemning his son to the same treadmill. In any case at this time it was the natural order of things for a boy in the Potteries. One of the ugliest features of the Industrial Revolution was the mass employment of young children of both sexes in factories and workshops. For generations children had worked below ground in the mines and in cottage industries, bringing home a badly-needed pittance for their parents. The first impact of the Revolution was felt in those rural valleys of the north where streams powered the early textile mills and pauper apprentices were shipped in by the wagon-load from the large cities to become little more than slave labour. When steam superseded water-power, the factories and mills moved into towns and villages where there were abundant supplies of coal nearby. The demand for labour, especially child labour, sucked in great numbers of families from the surrounding countryside whose means of livelihood in many cases had virtually disappeared as a result of the new technology. The scale of child labour in the expanding factories of the Workshop of the World was now of quite a different order. The appalling conditions under which thousands of these small children worked — the long hours, the high accident rate, the brutal treatment — move us today as perhaps no other manifestation of the Industrial Revolution. It is difficult for us to come to terms with the practice of employing children, some as young as four or five, under the harshest of regimes where their lives tended to be nasty, brutish and short.

George now entered one of the most ancient of industries. Because he spent much of his life in it in various capacities, something must be said here about the nature of the brick-yards and the conditions under which the employees then worked. At this time bricks were still made by hand as they had been for thousands of years. Although the first patent for a clay working machine was granted as early as 1619, mechanisation did not take the place of hand moulding until the middle of the nineteenth century and even then many small establishments using traditional methods continued to operate for many years afterwards. Certainly the usual method of making bricks while George Smith worked at Peake's was by hand.

Bricks are made from clay and fired in a kiln. Clay fortunately is found in many areas and there are brick-works scattered throughout the country. Bricks are often identified by colour and location, like English cheeses, and so we find such names as Leicester reds, Staffordshire blues etc. The clays used for brick making range from soft and plastic surface deposits to hard windstones, shales and marls. But for hand moulded bricks, clays with a high degree of plasticity are needed. Clay is usually obtained, or won, from quarries and pits. Once the top soil and vegetation is removed, the clay is dug out by hand. It is not often found in a pure state and the mineral impurities must first be eliminated by washing. Then, before the clay can be used, it has to be tempered with water and made in to a paste of uniform consistency. In Smith's day this final process was carried out either by kneading the clay with bare feet or, more usually, in a pug mill. The pug mill was a vertical cylinder of wood or iron with a shaft from which projected a spiral of horizontal knives. The tempered clay was inserted at the top of the cylinder, cut and thoroughly mixed by the knives, and then extruded from the base, ready for working or moulding.

Children were employed to carry the tempered clay from the pug mill to the brickmakers or moulders who worked at moulding benches in covered sheds. Though moulders could be men or women, the moulder was usually

Facing page: Children at the Pug Mill

a woman between twenty and thirty years old. She took a lump of clay and threw it into the mould which she had previously dipped in sand or water to prevent the clay brick from sticking to it. The mould was a simple wooden one and it was the usual, but not invariable, practice to use only one single brick mould at a time. She rammed the clay well into the mould using a mallet or a flat board with a handle fixed to it to force it home into the corners. She struck off the surplus clay by drawing some form of straight edge called a 'strike' across the top of the mould. The brick, weighing some eleven pounds, was then carried by a child and placed on a pallet or rack on the drying floor to dry and harden sufficiently to be handled. Children were also normally used to carry the 'green' (unfired) bricks to the kiln where they helped to pile them inside. Kilns were either circular with a domed roof or rectangular with an arched roof, with a tall chimney rising above them to produce the necessary draught. When the kiln was full a fire was lit in the fire chamber beneath it using wood faggots or coal. The heat increased slowly until the finishing temperature was reached. After staying for a certain time at the finishing temperature, the kiln was allowed to cool until the bricks could be handled by the drawers, who were responsible for emptying the kilns and sorting, stacking and loading the finished product. Small children were widely used for entering the kilns, and for removing and stacking the bricks. Tiles, incidentally, are of nearly the same composition as bricks and were usually fired in the same kiln protected by a screen of bricks to prevent them warping in the heat. An accurate picture of the organisation of a small brick-yard and the type of work carried out by the various age groups employed there has come down to us from a manufacturer of the more enlightened kind:

> I am a brick and tile manufacturer and sanitary pipemaker, in the neighbourhood of Tipton, midway between Birmingham and Wolverhampton. I employ about 50 work people, one half of whom are women and children. On principle, I am, however, opposed to the employment of women and children in clay works, and have made many efforts to dispense with their labour, but have always found insuperable obstacles in that direction.
>
> Our system of working is much the same as in all similar clay works in the South Staffordshire mining district; but the great demand for youths between from 14 to 18 years of age in the iron-works and collieries, compels the clay manufacturers to resort to the employment of girls, women and the younger lads. Hence girls of 9 or 10 years of age

and boys of 9 find work with us readily. These are mostly engaged in carrying clay to the moulding benches, carrying bricks and tiles off to the drying sheds, and again from the sheds to the kilns or ovens, besides numerous other odd jobs such as clearing away the scoriae and ashes from the kilns, ovens, drying sheds and engine, oiling the press dies and moulds, &c., carrying bricks, tiles, and pipes to and from the presses and stamps, sweeping and clearing out the rubbish from the sheds, kilns, and clay store rooms, and taking the clay to the pug-mills and carrying it away again to the store rooms or to the moulders as it may be required.

A brick-yard child

The younger children who carry clay to the moulders remove on average, 20 to 40 lbs. of clay on the head and about 10 to 20 lbs. in their arms. The older clay carriers are usually 14 to 16 years of age and carry a load of clay on the head and in the arms of 60 lbs. weight. Those who carry away the bricks from the moulders are mostly girls from 9 to 12 years old. They carry 10 lbs. of clay, plus a mould weighing 4 lbs. at each journey, say 2,000 times a day. So they each remove in one day of ten hours' work over 16 tons. The children who carry clay to the tile and quarry front brick and best goods moulders, have comparatively light work; say, for girls 10 to 13 years old an average of 5 tons of clay.

Here I have only referred to my own particular manufactory though what is true of these works is a fair average of all.

At last, their day's labour ended, the children would stumble wearily from the brick-yard hardly able to put one foot in front of another to enjoy a two mile walk home to a meagre supper.

During his years at Peake's Tileries George Smith was to perform the whole range of these activities. He has left us some details of his daily labours in the brick-yard. At the age of nine he was employed carrying about forty pounds of clay from the pug-mill to the moulding table. When there was no clay available, he had to carry the same weight of bricks. He did this, with brief breaks for food, for thirteen hours a day. Sometimes he had to work all night at the kilns. He recounts (and he was to tell this story many, many times during his life) how on one occasion, after his day's work was done, he had to carry 1200 nine-inch bricks from the moulding table to the drying floor. He estimated that he walked fourteen miles that night and that the total amount of clay he shifted was five and a half tons. And for this he received sixpence!

We also have a rather more imaginative account of aspects of life in a brickfield as they appeared to an experienced and impartial observer. Elihu Burritt, an interesting character, provides us with a vivid Doré-like picture of conditions there. He was an American known as 'the learned blacksmith' because of his devotion, after his labours at the forge, to the study of many European, Oriental and classical languages. He later became an ardent advocate of the doctrines of the Peace Society, seeking the settlement of international problems by peaceful meansand he played a prominent part in several Peace Congresses. Burritt lived in England for some years and from 1865 to 1870 he was the American Consul at Birmingham; thus being ideally placed for visiting brick-fields and canals. His book, *Walks in the Black Country* (Law, 1869), although published twenty years after Smith's exper-iences, presents us with aspects of life in a large brick-yard unchanged since Smith's childhood, even though the brick-yard Burritt visited was obviously more modern and better equipped than Peake's Tileries.

An exhausted oven girl

Meeting an extensive brick-maker, we stopped to see his establishment near the Old Hill Station, but a little way from Halesowen. He was carrying on a large business in the manufacture of blue-black bricks of every size and pattern for coping of walls, stable floors and other uses. The average hours of labour are from six a.m. to six p.m., and the wages paid to the young girls, mostly nine to twelve years old, vary from 8d. to 10d. per day, according to the amount of work they are able to perform, for the piece-work system generally prevails in the brick-yards.

We saw some of these young girls at work at the moulding bench, and watched with special interest the several parts they performed. A middle-aged woman, as we took her to be from some dress indications of her sex, was standing at the bench, butter stick in hand. Apparently she had on only a single garment reaching to her feet and this was so bespattered and weighted with wet clay that she resembled some marble statue clad in thin drapery. She wore a turban on her head of the same colour; for only one colour or consistency was possible at her work. The only thing feminine in her appearance was a pair of ear-drops as a token of her sex and of its tastes under any circumstances. With two or three moulds she formed the clay dough into loaves with wonderful tact and celerity. With a dash, splash and a blow one was perfectly shaped. One little girl then took it away and laid it down upon the drying floor with the greatest precision to keep the rows in perfect line. Another girl, a little older. brought the clay to the bench. This was a heavier task, and we watched her appearance and movements very closely. She was a girl apparently about thirteen. Washed and well clad, and with a little sportive life in her, she would have been almost pretty in face and form. But though there was some colour in her cheeks, it was the flitting flush of exhaustion. She moved in a kind of swaying, sliding way, as if muscle and joint did not fit and act together naturally. She first took up a mass of cold clay, weighing about twenty-five pounds, upon her head, and while balancing it there, she squatted to the heap without bending her body, and took up a mass of equal weight with both hands against her stomach, and with the two burdens walked about a rod and deposited them on the moulding bench. No wonder, we thought, that the colour in her cheeks was an unhealthy flush. With a mass of cold clay held against her stomach, and bending under another on her head, for ten or twelve hours in a day, it seemed a marvel that there could be any red blood in her veins at all. Each moulding woman has two, sometimes three, of these girls to serve her, one to bring the clay, the other to carry away the bricks when formed. Whether in cruel or good-natured satire, they are called 'pages', as if waiting upon a queen. A woman with her two or three pages will mould 3,000 bricks in a day by extra exertion; she is paid 2s. 8d. per thousand. Out of this she pays about 2s. per day to the girls that serve her; so she can easily earn large wages at this man's work, when well hardened to it, with requisite skill.

As we were leaving the last moulding shed we visited, a little boy came up to the bench who was but a little taller than one of its legs. I

Children counting their wages

asked him his age, and was surprised when he said he was seventeen. I almost mechanically put my umbrella up against him, and found he exceeded its length by full nine inches; so that he must have been quite three feet and a half on his bare feet although he at first looked shorter. He had probably found no other time to grow except when a-bed at night or on the Sunday. This enterprising manufacturer makes the hardest and best bricks to be found in the market. The canal passes close to his kilns on one side and the railway on the other; so that he has ready and cheap means of transporting them in any direction or to any distance in the country.

Smith's early years in the brick-yard were to have a searing and enduring effect on his mind and character. His experience was similar to that of Charles Dickens in the blacking factory, except that he was exposed to it for all his boyhood years and beyond. Physically exhausting as the work was for children and young people, Smith felt strongly that the poisonous moral atmosphere in the brick-yards was equally degrading. He had experienced this at first hand and its squalid and brutalising nature, so utterly contrary to his Christian upbringing, left an indelible impression upon him. It had the same effect on a small number of concerned manufacturers who confirmed the truth of Smith's comments. One manufacturer from Tipton who reluctantly employed a number of women and girls in his yard, testified to the demoralising effects of the mixed employment of the sexes:

> A flippancy and familiarity of manners with boys and men grows daily on the young girls. Then, the want of respect and delicacy towards females exhibits itself in every act, word and look; for the lads grow so precocious, and the girls so coarse in their language and manners from close companionship at work, that... they sing unblushingly before all the

lewdest and most disgusting songs. The overtime work is still more objectionable because boys and girls, men and women, are less under the watchful eye of the master, nor looked upon by the eye of day. All these things, the criminality, levity, coarse phrases, sinful oaths, lewd gestures, and conduct of the adults and youths, exercise a terrible influence for evil on the young children. It is quite common for girls employed in brick yards to have illegitimate children. Of the thousands whom I have met with, or known as working, I should say that one in every four who had arrived at the age of twenty had had an illegitimate child. Several had had three or four.

Writing about this aspect of brick-yard life some years later, Smith went even further and condemned "the matter-of-course falling in with the most profligate of indulgences — the open turning aside of mere boys and girls in order to have intercourse, the setting on to it of such by the men, and the meeting with a roar by men and women of the discovery of such."

That this moral squalor was not merely confined to the brick-yards but was rife in the factories and mills is revealed in the testimony of other writers and reformers of the time. Peter Gaskell (1806-41), in his book, *Artisans and Machinery*, examined the moral and physical condition of factory workers and concluded that "the bringing together numbers of the young of both sexes in factories, has been a prolific source of moral delinquency. The stimulus of a heated atmosphere, the contact of opposite sexes, the example of license upon the animal passions — all have conspired to produce a very early development of sexual appetencies [desires]." It was in this environment and under these appalling working conditions that Smith spent his childhood, adolescence and early manhood. It is a wonder that he, too, was not corrupted and the desire to better himself extinguished. For this he had the influence of his home to thank.

The Cry of the Brick-Yard Children

Is there no pity, in country or city,
For the poor little brick-maker lad?
'Mid the bricks and the clay, he toils all the day,
And often his young heart is sad.
Less kind words than blows his master bestows,
Upon the hapless young drudge,
Who must wearily run, 'neath the pitiless sun,
'Till he reels — and yet mustn't mudge.

Oh God! who hast moulded mankind, and enfolded
A spirit undying in clay,
Let man not erase all childhood's sweet grace,
That rivals the lambkins at play.
By toil's weary round, [Thine image is ground]
From hearts that are pliable yet.
Accurs'd is the gain, wrung from infancy's pain,
That coin'd from infancy's sweat.

On the altar of pelf the high priesthood of self—
The heathen of Britain — do lay,
The children; Oh spare! the innocents there;
Smite the hands uplifted to slay
The mind ere it's grown, the soul ere it's known
The beauty and freshness of earth!
The blossoms of youth, the seedlings of truth,
Should not be chok'd up at birth.

From the brick-yards a cry goes up to the sky,
"Are there none to pity and save?
Who dare boldly demand, throughout our good land,
The freedom of the brick-yard slave?"
The lambs of God's fold, as Israel of old,
'Gainst the breakers of His righteous law,
In piteous tone, to Him make their moan,
"Must we still make bricks without straw?"

Anon

Chapter 3: Prelude to Coalville

O put not your trust in princes, nor in any child of man.
Psalm 146

Smith was determined that he would not be dragged down like the other boys but would escape from the bondage of the brick-yards and make something of his life. Education was the key and during the winter when the brick-yards and the canal were frozen up and work was impossible, George seized the chance to attend school. In addition, between the ages of fifteen and seventeen, he went to a night school four times a week. He paid his fees out of the money he earned by watching over the brick-kilns all night for two nights a week for several years. Of the shilling he received, sixpence went to the schoolmaster and the other sixpence he spent on books.

Among those he bought and studied were Bunyan's *Holy War,* Defoe's *Robinson Crusoe*, Cobbett's *Advice to Young Men,* Chambers *Information for the People,* and Goldsmith's *History of the Earth and Animated Nature* — a curious collection but no doubt informative. It is not too dissimilar from the small collection of books Hardy gives to Gabriel Oak in *Far from the Madding Crowd.*

Smith was sustained in his efforts by his family background and the influence of the chapel. His parents were committed Wesleyan Methodists and he grew up in a domestic environment of piety and Sunday observance. The principles of Methodism formed his character and were the bedrock upon which his activities were based throughout his life. As an adult he would wholeheartedly accept the emphasis on practical charity, a concern for the material as well as the spiritual welfare of the poor, the need to make known the Gospel and to stress the love and pity of God. As a lay member, Smith could expect to share with the ministry the tasks of preaching the Gospel as widely and as persuasively as possible, caring for his fellow Christians and helping to run the chapel's affairs.

Despite his arduous six day working week, Smith regularly attended Sunday School and later began attending chapel services with his parents. As he entered his teens he could not help becoming aware that, even in Tunstall, he was growing up in an atmosphere, originally of internal nonconformist controversy, but now one of highly-charged religious rivalry between the Methodists of the Old Connexion (the Wesleyans) and those of the new Connexion (the Primitive Methodists).

Primitive Methodism had its roots in a reaction against the comatose condition into which Wesleyan Methodism had drifted. At the end of the eighteenth century Methodism had lost its sharp cutting edge and the revivalist spirit was already on the wane even before the death of John Wesley in 1791. Methodists had for many years earned a reputation for sobriety, thrift and industry but these virtues, without the fierce evangelical fire, had led them into a cosy respectability. Methodism, in fact, had become a middle-class conservative institution, mainly interested in the undemanding task of self-organisation and preserving the status quo.

There were still many, however, in whom the flame still burned and they found their leaders in two gifted and eloquent men, Hugh Bourne and William Clowes. Expelled from the Methodist Society for their unorthodox views and activities, in 1810 they formed the Society of Primitive Methodists, a mission marked by strong emphasis on conversion and salvation. The period 1812 to 1843 saw a rapid expansion of the new sect as a kind of native missionary organisation. Enthusiasts spread the message through the Potteries and the Black Country to the East and West Midlands while others carried the torch into Yorkshire and northward to Durham and Northumberland.

The splitting of the Methodists into the Old and New Connexions was the cause of bitter dissension and rivalry for years. The impact made by Primitive Methodism on a small community can be seen in Tunstall. Here in 1808 the Wesleyan Methodist church had some 400 members; by 1811 they had lost one half of them, and half the Sunday School as well, to the Primitive Methodists.

As he grew older, Smith persuaded many 'street and pot bank' boys and girls to join the Sunday School and when he was seventeen, Smith became a teacher there himself. The Methodist Sunday Schools had already established a tradition of attracting men and women from modest backgrounds with burgeoning gifts of oratory, leadership and organisation. The Sunday Schools gave them training and experience and offered them the scope to realise their potential. Such was the case with Smith. The keen, articulate brick-yard worker was soon marked out as one of the coming men and a little later he became one of the founders of the Young Men's Mutual Improvement Society attached to the chapel. The young men used to meet to discuss moral, social and religious topics and George, growing more confident, read two essays before the group, one entitled 'Youth, the Best Time for Improvement' and the other, 'Knowledge'.

Meanwhile, he had been making progress in the brick-yard. He had graduated from the clay heap to the moulder's table and from there to a junior supervisory post. He had rapidly developed into a skilled and capable employee, and his employers realised that they had a serious-minded, hard-working and trustworthy young man in their yard. By the time Smith was twenty one there was little about the practical side of brickmaking he did not know and he had learned a considerable amount about the nature of clay deposits and the uses to which the various types of clay could be put. He was also beginning to manifest an original and inventive cast of mind.

In the chapel there was a young teacher called Mary Mayfield; Mary had been born in Tunstall on 12th March 1828, the daughter of a hawker, and had spent her life there. Although nearly three years older than George she was attracted by her earnest young colleague and recognised the potential in what was undoubtedly a very superior working man. George was similarly attracted to Mary whose views were so close to his own and he asked her to be his wife. George's parents approved of his choice indeed, they could hardly have wished for a better match for their eldest son, and on 1st November 1852 George and Mary were married at the Parish Church in Tunstall. Like most young working-class women of her time, Mary was unable to write, so she simply made her cross on the marriage certificate.

They were not to stay in Clayhills for very long. In 1854, about eighteen months after their marriage, they decided to leave the close-knit community in which they had both grown up and the chapel that played such a prominent part in their lives. Smith was growing increasingly restive over the workers' conditions in Peake's Tileries. He had spoken out more than once about the abuses going on there and he probably felt he could expect little further advancement or opportunity under Peake. He was ambitious and he wanted to broaden his experience. As a first-class worker, one with a good name and character, he felt he would have no difficulty in finding a more responsible job. This would be the first step on the way to starting his own small business.

Smith found employment in a brick-yard owned by a Harry West in the hamlet of Ladderedge (or Laddridge as it is called locally), at that time a cluster of cottages and farm buildings about two miles south of Leek. The brick-yard lay about three quarters of a mile to the west on the side of a steepish hill overlooking Leek and the Churnet valley. The remains of West's brick-field can still be seen on the right-hand side of the A53 as you travel from Leek to Longsdon. Although none of the brick-field buildings survive, it is difficult to disguise the activities of the extractive process. West, who was also a farmer, a not uncommon combination in the district, lived a mile from his works at Wall Grange, a large farmhouse built on a hillside in a bend of the river Churnet. It looked down, as it does today, on the branch of the Caldon Canal that runs up to the southern edge of Leek. The canal ended in a wharf adjoining the railway station and here the young couple found lodgings "in the further of the two cottages near the Leek wharf opposite to Woodcroft". Today Woodcroft is a built-up area and nothing remains of the cottage where Smith and his wife lived.

While working for West, Smith gave the first sign of his innovative talent. He made the first blue bricks and sanitary ware ever produced in that neighbourhood. His blue bricks were made from clays found in Staffordshire and the West Midlands which contained about ten per cent iron. He also made the pipes which carried the water from a spring to West's house. Despite enjoying the confidence of his employer, Smith did not stay long in Ladderedge. He had saved a little money and he was keen to strike out on his own when an opportunity presented itself. He did not have to wait long. It so happened that during his travels in the district he had discovered at Reapsmoor the existence of a suitable clay stratum close to the surface. This was the spur he needed.

He parted with West on friendly terms, helped his wife pack up their belongings, and set off for Reapsmoor, an isolated hamlet a thousand feet up on the edge of the Derbyshire moors, some seven miles north-east of Leek and two and a half miles south of Longnor. Taking the Buxton road out of Leek, Smith and his wife toiled up the hill before turning off up the steep narrow road to Thorncliffe. On their left rose the Roaches and the strange shapes of Hen Cloud and Ramshaw Rocks. The road climbed steadily until they reached the Mermaid Inn and they soon found themselves on the sparsely populated Derbyshire plateau. It is a bleak and desolate landscape, especially in winter. Reapsmoor itself lies in a shallow, saucer-shaped depression which provides some protection from the weather and a welcome contrast to the forbidding moorlands. It was, and remains, a collection of isolated farm houses and cottages a mile to the west of the Manifold valley.

This was the place where Smith had chosen to start a small brick and tile yard on his own account. They settled into a cottage, their first real home, and here they agreed later they spent the happiest years of their married life. The cottage was to provide Smith with vivid memories which he was to treasure all his life. The district has hardly changed during the intervening century and a half; even today there is little traffic to disturb the quiet of the farming community. It is interesting to find that evidence of Smith's first venture is still there. The remains of his brick-field lie on the left as you go up the short road that leads from the dairy at the Longnor/Warslow crossroads to the old school and chapel. The field from which Smith won his clay is close to a farm, and a house and cottages overlook the grassy hollows where he laboured.

Their cottage stood about three hundred yards past the present school house on the Reapsmoor to Longnor Road. It has now virtually disappeared but traces of it can still be made out on the left hand side of the road. Opposite a large farm, within a rough triangle enclosed by a low stone wall, are a number of trees. This, according to local sources, was the site of Smith's cottage.

Smith worked hard at his new venture for he was resolved to make a success of it. As he had done at Ladderedge, he introduced blue bricks to the district and he also produced glazed ware and roof tiles. No wares like these were obtainable within twenty miles. He began by having his goods carried by cart to Buxton. This proved to be a difficult journey over exposed roads that were poor at the best of times and frequently impassable in the winter. Transport for his wares became a major problem. He was miles from the Buxton to Ashbourne railway and there was no canal in the area. This also made coal for his kiln expensive. Smith could hardly have failed to be aware of this when he set up his business but he certainly under-estimated his fuel costs.

Smith was not the man to be deterred by difficulties nor was he one to compromise his principles. He pressed on and, remembering the vile conditions under which he and thousands of young children like him had toiled in the brick-fields of the Potteries, he determined to do what he could to improve working conditions in his own brick and tile yard and to protect those who had neither the spirit nor the education to raise themselves from abject poverty and squalor. He was now his own master and from the start he set his face against employing boys under the age of thirteen and he steadfastly refused to employ girls and women at all.

His early years had centred around regular Sunday attendance and chapel activities. Now Sunday School work was to become one of the cornerstones of his activities for the next twenty years. So it is no surprise to find that, despite the increasing pressures of his business, in 1856 he started a Wesleyan Sunday School in the pleasant two-storied building not far up the road from his cottage. He became its first superintendent and cared for the group of poor children he collected there twice every Sunday. This year was to be a particularly happy one for Smith because on the 3rd April his wife, to his great joy, bore him a son. They called him George after his father; his birth certificate shows the single Christian name, although he was sometimes called George Mayfield later on. Smith often referred sentimentally in his diaries and books to that 'old ivy-covered cottage' where his family grew up.

The months passed happily enough as Smith laboured in his brick-yard, but he finally realised that he stood little chance of developing his business in such an isolated area with all its transport difficulties. He began to explore other possibilities. One day in 1857 he saw an advertisement in a Staffordshire paper for a manager to take sole charge of a large brick and tile works at Humberstone, a hamlet to the west of Leicester. He applied for the post; the owners were impressed by the experience and the confidence of the young brickmaker and decided to offer him the post at a salary of £125 per annum.

He settled his family into a pleasant lodge called Queen's Cottage not far from his new yard and then began to improve production and put the business on a sound financial footing. The owners' confidence in Smith was not misplaced, even though he was only to stay with them for less than two years. While at Humberstone he managed the works with such skill and ability that, for the first time in its history, the business produced substantial profits for the owners. Smith achieved this without having to employ children, young girls or women. He continued his Reapsmoor policy of not allowing young people to work overtime or to do night work. He thus made his point to other employers in the district that commercial success in the brick-fields did not depend on the exploitation of children at starvation wages. As usual, he was active from the beginning in Sunday School affairs and finding a gap in provision he founded a Wesleyan Sunday School near his home.

Further opportunities beckoned. From time to time he used to travel back to Clayhills and Tunstall to see his parents and his friends at the chapel. Smith was a keen and experienced observer of landscape and on his journeys he examined the land about him with an eye to what might lie beneath the surface. His road home led him through the straggling mining village of

Coalville. Looking at the remains of the old bell pits and the slag-heaps from the collieries, Smith wondered if valuable seams of fire, terracotta and other clays might lie under the surface. Although successful and valued at Humberstone, he was still only the manager there and he was anxious to set up in business on his own account again. He seized his chance when he heard early in 1859 that a small red brick and drain pipe yard was shortly becoming available in Coalville. This yard was capable of employing three or four hands and belonged to the Whitwick Colliery Company. It was not a yard producing bricks and tiles for sale in the open market; most of its products were taken up by the colliery company. Smith saw its possibilities and immediately applied to the proprietors who agreed, verbally, to let it to him for £40 per annum.

Before the agreement was actually signed, Smith investigated the yard further. He discovered it contained valuable seams of clay which had not been tested or used. He at once had samples of possible products made up and these indicated that a class of goods such as ornamental tiles, white bricks, red terra-cotta, sanitary ware, blue bricks and tiles, quarries (i.e. plain tiles) and tiles of various colours, shapes and sizes, and various types of architectural moulding could be made. He saw the opportunity of developing a new trade in Leicestershire and the Midlands. Smith was more determined than ever to prove two points. First, that quality products could be manufactured profitably without employing boys under thirteen or girls under sixteen. Secondly, that acceptable wares could be produced at a profit from clays which other brickfield owners considered useless.

Smith, bursting with enthusiasm and his head filled with ideas for the future, then proceeded to commit a grievous error. His action was in accord with his trusting and impetuous nature, but it was to have repercussions upon him and and his family for many years. Without further ado, he decided to resign his post at Humberstone. When his employers heard of his intention, they were so reluctant to lose their vigorous and effective manager that they offered him another £50 per annum to stay. But Smith's mind was made up and he refused their offer.

He took some samples of the goods made out of his newly-discovered clay into Coalville and, without bothering to ensure his contract was signed, he showed them to two of the partners of the Whitwick Colliery Company. As he did so, Smith relates that "something told me that I had made a mistake, a tremendous mistake." He certainly had. The partners were impressed; so impressed, in fact, that after a consultation in private they decided to withdraw from the proposed contract. They returned to inform Smith they were retaining control of the yard after all but would be happy to employ him as manager at a salary of £75 per annum. Poor Smith felt as though the ground had suddenly opened up under his feet. He had given up a post paying him £125 per annum and he now found himself unemployed and with a wife and two small children to keep. He was utterly at a loss; his normal confidence and power of speech deserted him; meekly he accepted their offer.

It seems strange that Smith accepted this miserable situation. It is almost as though he was so overwhelmed by the duplicity of the men he was dealing with that, like Billy Budd, he could find no words of protest suitable for the occasion. It is as though the honest, straight-dealing Smith, whose word was his bond, was almost paralysed by the shock of encountering deceit of this nature. Presumably he could have asked his employers at Humberstone to allow him to withdraw his resignation. We know they were most reluctant to lose him and they would have been unlikely to cavil at a technicality. Managers of the calibre of Smith were far from common. Again, even if Smith, a proud and stubborn man, did not relish the role of suppliant or if there were other factors unknown to us, there were surely posts in the industry he might have sought as a temporary measure. He had a little money saved from his two years at Humberstone which he could have used as a cushion.

Smith returned to Humberstone a disillusioned man and shamefully confessed to his wife how he had been outwitted by the unscrupulous owners of the Whitwick Colliery Company who were now his new employers. Mary, as usual, was sympathetic and supportive; she urged him to put this misfortune behind him and think of their future together in Coalville. They now had another son, Charles Henry, born a few days into the New Year, whose arrival only served to heighten Smith's concern for his family's security.

A few days later Smith took his leave of the proprietors and the hands in the brickworks at Humberstone with whom he had worked so harmoniously. With a heavy heart and a sense of foreboding he found hard to disguise, he set about moving his family to Coalville.

Chapter 4: Drama and Dissention

"Coalville on a wet day is a gruesome sight".
Shell Guide to Leicestershire

In the early part of the nineteenth century Coalville was known simply as 'Long Lane', a narrow country road with a few houses scattered on either side of it. The area formed part of the Leicestershire and South Derbyshire coalfield and mining had been carried on locally since mediaeval times. It was a small scale industry, partly because of the problem of carrying coal by pack-horse on the difficult roads of the period. In 1822 a mining engineer, William Stenson, sank a successful mine in the parish of Whitwick; in 1824 the Whitwick Colliery Company was established and within a few years coal was being produced in quantity to meet an increasing demand from Leicester. Stenson built himself a new house (now demolished) next to the present Municipal Offices and called it, unsurprisingly, Coalville House. It seems fairly certain that this unlovely name was adopted for a growing village of some twelve hundred souls.

Stenson now ran into the high cost of carrying bulk quantities of coal by road to Leicester and became the prime mover in developing the Leicester and Swannington railway link. He surveyed the route himself, went to Liverpool in 1828 and had it approved by George Stephenson, who was working on the Liverpool to Manchester railway and engaged his son Robert Stephenson as engineer for the line. The line was opened both for coal and passenger traffic in 1833 and the benefits were immediate. The price of coal in Leicester plummeted. Coal brought by canal from Derbyshire and sold at sixteen shillings per ton could not compete with coal of the same quality carried from Whitwick Colliery by rail at ten shillings per ton.

Originally there was only a halt at Long Lane but the building of the Railway Hotel swiftly followed. This housed the booking office in its front room while a bell on the back of the front door was rung to signal the arrival of a train. Coalville station, which played such a prominent part in Smith's future journeys, came later.

Robert Stephenson was much impressed by the success of Stenson's

Whitwick Colliery. Like Smith, he had an experienced eye and he spotted the potential for coal-mining and brickmaking in the neighbouring Snibston Estate. When it came on the market in 1831 he persuaded his father to buy it and together they developed a major and profitable colliery. George Stephenson came to live at Alton Grange on the road from Coalville to Ashby-de-la-Zouch (his old house is still there) and he and his son, with their enlightened views on colliery management, proved, like Stenson, considerable benefactors to the inhabitants.

While developing his mine, Stenson had become aware of the rich clay deposits in the locality and in 1828 established a small Brick and Tile Yard, later known as the Whitwick Colliery Brick and Tile Works. It was to this yard and to this growing industrial village that Smith came with his family in 1859, the year that Robert Stephenson died. He had exchanged his house at Humberstone for "a three-roomed, dark, dirty, low, unpicturesque, barrack-looking cottage, or hovel, enveloped in the fumes and smoke of a lime and refuse spoil-bank". It was all he could afford, given his modest salary. Smith, to his chagrin, now found himself manager where he had expected to be a proprietor, and he started his new job in an atmosphere clouded by suspicion and distrust. In due course another storm would break upon him and plunge his family into a period of grinding and heart-breaking poverty, but this was still below the horizon.

Smith quickly settled down as manager of the works, determined to make the best of things. Intent on providing security and a better life for his wife and young sons, he proceeded with his usual vigour and ingenuity to show his new masters what kind of a man they had engaged. Smith brought his Reapsmoor and Humberstone practices into operation and insisted from the start that that no boys under the age of twelve should be employed in the yard, nor any girls or women, and that no child should be allowed to work overtime or on Sundays. He also taught the young lads how to make a new class of moulded and terra-cotta goods which he had designed for high-class work in mansions, churches, chapels and public buildings, so they might begin to take pride in their work and be ambitious for the future. The new range of products was later reflected in the full title of the works: The Whitwick Colliery Company's Terra Metallic Tileries, Ornamental White Brick and Sewage Pipe Works.

At the same time he sought out new markets and new customers in the area and the business began to blossom under his aggressive management. His efforts and success, as is so often the case, also brought jealousy and malice in their train. Smith was not the man to brook delays or to go round about and his directness and lack of tact made him unpopular. The new broom aroused the latent hostility of a particular official at the Colliery Company whom he calls Killimsharp.

About two years after his arrival the bad feeling between them flared up and there was a violent quarrel. For what happened next we are indebted to his booklet, *An Open Letter to my Friends*, written some thirty years later. Even writing so long after the event Smith's bitterness over the sharp practice of the colliery company and their subsequent treatment of him comes through his narrative very strongly. It is a curious booklet for two reasons. First, it is written in Smith's high style, impassioned and hectic, and the reader must come to terms with constant exaggeration and a deep-seated sense of injustice. Secondly, in his narrative, the names of firms and places in and around Coalville (which he calls Bosvil) are thinly disguised, while he gives ingenious sobriquets to those he came into conflict with e.g. Messrs. Catchimquick, Squeezimtite, Keepimlow, Blindim and Killimsharp. One might claim this booklet is more a caustic commentary on his hostile treatment by the people of Coalville than an attempt to put the record straight. One also senses that, in some instances, it is a case of *qui s'excuse, s'accuse*.

It is difficult now to identify these characters with any certainty. What is certain, however, is that Catchimquick was James Whetstone, one of the well-known Whetstone family of Leicester. He lived at Springfield House in Coalville, a property which Smith was to buy several years later after Whetstone's death. He and Smith quickly became reconciled and Whetstone was to give £25 towards the building of Smith's new schoolroom. Another of those involved was probably William Stenson Jnr., a director of the Whitwick Colliery, whose family were business associates of the Whetstones during this period.

In his dramatic account of the incident, Smith appears to be saved from a violent death, if not by divine intervention, at least by some support given to his good right arm by a Higher Hand:

> After I had been up nearly all one night superintending the burning of a kiln of special goods, I had retired to rest awhile until daylight. I had not been in bed very long before a man from the works came puffing and panting at my bedroom door, stating that all the men in the yard had struck, not for a rise in wages, but against me, the leaders of whom had

been paid 2/6 and in other cases 1/- by one of the leading cement officials to do so, or in other words to hound me out of the neighbourhood.

I hastened to the Coal and Cement Offices with books and papers in my hands, and as I neared the top of a large flight of brick steps, outside the offices, a dark, tall, 'dandy cock' man Mr. Killimsharp — rushed at me with all his might to push me backwards to the bottom of the steps — in fact, to break my back — but I gave myself — or a Higher Hand did for me — a twist, and nothing but my hat, books and spectacles fell to the bottom. This was in the presence of several men in the offices, and others outside on the ground

This murderous onslaught on me brought forth the dormant courage, nerve, and pluck in me, and, in face of death and his threats, I struggled and fought my way step by step to the top of the landing, neither vanquished or killed. He then tried his best to throw me over the parapet, but by this time he had found his match, and I took hold of him and said, 'If I must go over the wall, we shall both go together and see what the bottom is like'.

He let go his hold of me and backed into the office. I was no sooner at his heels in his den, telling him that he had made a fool of himself, than he began again to do his best to kill me, and for a time I did nothing more than keep him at arm's length, and give him a shaking by the collar. Poor fellow, he gnashed his teeth, clawed, kicked, and almost spat fire. He now saw that he was no match for me and for a brief spell ceased his Satanic work to get his breath, which I took as an indication that he was spent out, but which was not the case, for in an unguarded moment he ran at me with all the anger of a demon and, seizing the foreman's stout, strong and tough yard-stick out of his hand, he began to belabour my head with it. The stick was broken in several pieces, and I was dazed, but before the life was knocked out of me I got hold of him and said, 'It seems I am to be killed but I shall not be killed without a struggle for my life, so here goes'.

I took hold of him by the hair of his head — for I now felt as strong as Samson — and was about to dash his head upon the desk with my left hand, and to leave marks upon his face with my right one. His friends in the office saw that I had turned the tables upon him, and in their fear for his life rushed on me. I began to demolish them without any weapons — except justice, truth, and God on my side — and while they were flying to the door my would-be murderer began to cry peccavi. I left him completely vanquished, discomforted, and a sadder and wiser man, and proceeded with my work in quieting the men on the works.

This fracas at the works brought Catchimquick, the principal proprietor, out from Leicester by the first train the following morning to investigate. Catchimquick, who later came to be regarded as a friend by Smith, soon saw how matters lay, looked into the quarrel, found for Smith and offered to send Killimsharp packing. Smith, with his usual magnanimity restored, would have none of this but Catchimquick insisted that if Killimsharp remained in the business he would separate them physically and commercially. He told Smith that in future he should have sole charge of all business matters relating to the works which would be regarded as a separate firm. "Everything you have from the Coal and Cement Works must be paid for, and everything the Cement Company buys from your works must be paid for. All letters and correspondence, money orders, cheques and bankers' drafts must be made payable to you and pass through your hands, and you must also make out your own balance sheets". To this sensible solution Smith agreed and he promised not to speak to Killimsharp again. He was as good as his word and in fact he did not do so for the next eleven years while he was connected with the firm, although he goes out of his way to stress that he had forgiven Killimsharp over and over again for his wrongdoing.

It was not only in his business life that Smith made enemies. Soon after his arrival in Coalville he reviewed the evangelical scene and found it wanting. He started a Wesleyan Sunday School and within two years under his vigorous direction its numbers had grown from six to over sixty. He had introduced several extra teachers to help with the increased numbers and was both surprised and aggrieved when his teachers turned against him without warning and proposed and elected another leader in front of the whole Sunday School. This was too much for Smith who made a dignified exit, though he later confessed, with an unusual degree of self-knowledge, that he had, perhaps, been going rather too fast for his colleagues. "I took my two little sons by the hand and put on their caps, and with tears dropping down my face, we journied towards the plain of Mamre* to await the openings of Providence". This meant, in effect, that he severed his connection with the orthodox Wesleyan Methodists who had played so prominent a part throughout his life.

He did not have to wait long for a suitable opening. A few days later a deputation from the Primitive Methodist Sunday School Teachers called at his house and asked him to take charge of their Sunday School. Smith decided to throw in his lot with the new Connexion; the Superintendent

---

*A place two miles north of Hebron associated with Abraham and Isaac.

resigned in his favour and willingly agreed to serve as a teacher under him.

The new enterprise prospered like all Smith's evangelical work. But the expansion of his Sunday School endeavours and the growing demands of a now flourishing business made extra help imperative. Fortunately, Smith did not have to look far. Reinforcements for both activities were at hand in the shape of his father, William. We have seen that William Smith was an honest and diligent worker. Some years after his son left Tunstall William Smith followed his son's example and struck out on his own and started his own small business. This failed rather miserably; he was not in the same class as his son as an innovator and entrepreneur. His son obviously fathered the flattering comment in *Hanani* that William Smith's "improvement of mechanism and of material, and variations of traditional applications of clays, though unpatented, are in use all over the world" (sic), but this is the usual Smith hyperbole. So when in 1863 George Smith invited him (one has the impression that he was more or less summoned) to join him at Coalville, William promptly responded to the call. He relinquished his post as manager of a brick-yard in Derbyshire and moved with his wife to Coalville. Here he was employed by his son as under-manager at the works at 30/- per week, though this starting salary was to be gradually increased.

William's help in the Sunday School was to prove most valuable. The labourer from the brick-yard at Tunstall had grown considerably in another direction after his son had left the district. He felt drawn to a more evangelical role in the chapel and, despite some misgivings about his ability, he made a start with cottage prayer meetings and distributing tracts. Slowly he developed from a class leader into a local preacher. On his arrival in Coalville he was happy to join his son and the Primitive Methodists. His name as a local preacher appeared on what the Primitive Methodists called 'The Plan' or circuit, even though the Quarter Day Board, composed of several local preachers and other oficials, put his name on without consulting him.

During the next ten years, on six to eight Sundays in each quarter, William Smith went on foot to visit villages within a ten mile radius to preach the gospel. He used to take his concertina with him and advertise his arrival by singing and playing through the village streets to gather the people together for a service. He proved a more successful preacher than businessman, speaking straight from the heart to the type of audience whose background and aspirations he knew intimately — colliers, labourers, brick-yard workers and their families.

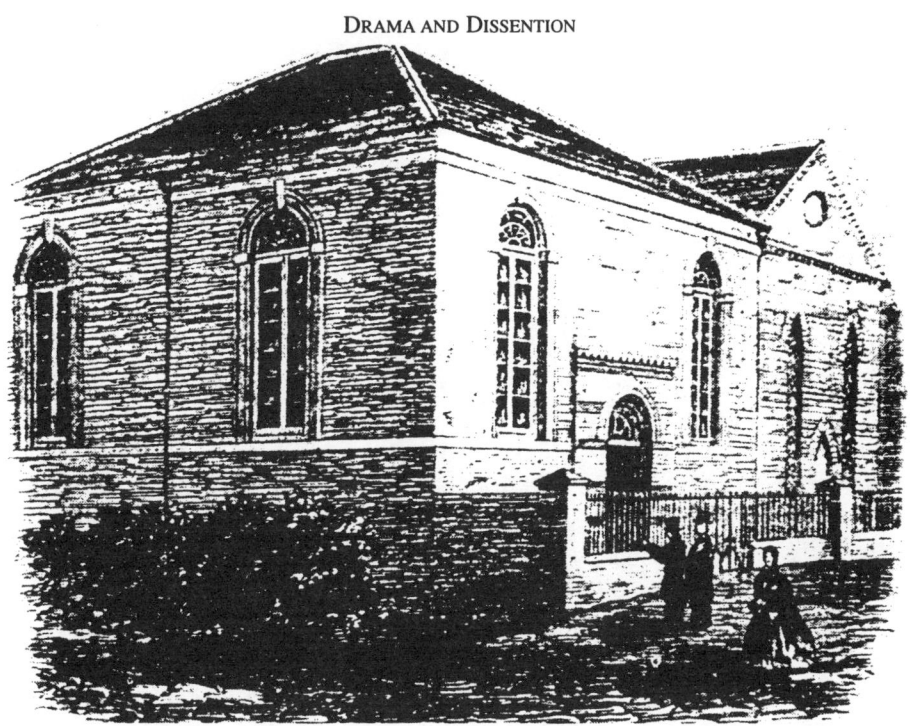

Coalville Primitive Methodist Chapel and Schoolroom

With his father's help, Smith's Sunday School continued to flourish, but there were breakers ahead. Neither Christ Church, the local Anglican church, nor the other Nonconformist chapels were enamoured of the Sunday School's popularity and, as a result of local jealousy and dissension, George Smith was curtly informed by the Church of England authorities who owned the building that the schoolroom would no longer be available to him. Like some Old Testament prophet, he shepherded his teachers and his flock now numbering over 180 into the Primitive Methodist Chapel itself and managed as best he could among the pews. So successful were Smith and his father that it became obvious that meetings crowded among the chapel pews could not continue. With characteristic energy, Smith set out to raise the money to build a new Sunday School next to the chapel and on 8th August 1865 he was given the privilege, as superintendent, of laying the foundation stone. (Today the site is occupied by business premises.)

He found the fund-raising hard going:

> The circuit and other officials and teachers were poor and had begun to 'fight shy' of the undertaking. I was now again almost single-handed

but by sticking to it and with the help and cheer of my wife, such as she was able to give, the project became a thorough success, except that a tremendous heavy debt rested upon my shoulders with no prospect of much local help being forthcoming.

Without wishing to belittle Smith's endeavours, he is being somewhat economical with the actualité here. The total cost of the schoolroom, including the erection of the new gallery on three sides of the chapel, palisading, lighting and the 'warming apparatus' came to about £430. All the materials for this Gothic-style building were supplied by the Whitwick Colliery Company and he received donations from local worthies. The colliery owners in the district had traditionally given land and money for the building of chapels and schools for the benefit of their colliers, many of whom had been brought down from the north-east because of their special skills. It was widely accepted that Methodism by its nature improved the behaviour and living standards of miners and other heavy manual labourers.

Smith was delighted with the results of his enterprise and the new schoolroom was much admired. It was 38 ft 6 ins by 21 ft 6 ins and two storeys in height. Both storeys had four classrooms, two at each end of a large centre room, with access into the chapel and gallery. The rooms were lit by tall narrow windows and the roof was covered with alternate rows of blue and red tiles.

The reference to the extent of his wife's help here — "such as she was able to give" —reflects the fact that during this eventful year Mary had begun to sicken. She had never properly recovered from the birth of their third son, Hollins Capper, two years before. Sadly, this little boy, like hundreds of thousands of Victorian children, was to die in childhood.

Meanwhile, even though he had only been in charge of the Coalville works for a few years, Smith's skilled management and the introduction of new methods and fresh products were producing excellent results for the owners. Smith achieved this progress without sacrificing or compromising his principles in any way. His balance sheet proved that it was quite possible to run a brick-yard profitably without recourse to the abuses that characterised the system. Few of the owners or managers in the district chose to follow his example. Instead, human nature being what it is, Smith became aware of a certain hostility towards him from local proprietors jealous of his success and irritated by his methods.

Despite his growing unpopularity, reports of his methods and aspirations filtered through to London. There they reached the ears of Robert Baker, one of Her Majesty's two Chief Inspectors of Factories and a minor and virtually forgotten figure in nineteenth century reform. Baker, born on 1803 in York, was the son of a surgeon and received medical training himself. In 1825 he was appointed Poor Law Medical Officer in Leeds where he was to work until 1858. In 1834 he became a Sub-inspector of Factories under Lord Shaftesbury's seminal Factories Act of 1833 in charge of a vast area covering Yorkshire, Nottinghamshire, Derbyshire and Lincolnshire. Baker and his colleagues were primarily concerned with law-enforcement, but they also had to submit regular reports to the Government on the state of the factory population, whether the new Act was operating correctly and to suggest any amendments to it they felt necessary. Later on they were required to make reports on particular subjects or industries and these reports made by impartial and experienced observers, together with their regular submissions, are a mine of information about industrial conditions during the Victorian age. More importantly, the reports were to act as a catalyst for legislation.

Baker himself was an unashamed 'Reformer' or Liberal, an active and fearless inspector who throughout his life championed the cause of the working classes. He was a formidable, down-to-earth character who did not suffer fools gladly or tolerate evasion of the law. He was, in fact, one of the early keepers of the Victorian social conscience. He had to contend with some flagrant abuses by the millowners and he found himself in and out of court for years bringing prosecutions under the various Factory Acts. The following example highlights the conditions under which some children were employed by unscrupulous owners. In 1838 Baker had found the Dewsbury firm of Taylor Ibbotson and Co. employing boys continuously from 6 a.m. on a Friday until 5 p.m. on the following day with breaks only for meals. What made matters worse was that their work, shoddy grinding, filled the air with so much dust they could hardly see one another three yards apart. In their defence the firm claimed that the boys had four hours rest in the night! The owners were duly convicted, but Baker commented to the Home Office that they had been let off far too lightly. He made himself so unpopular in the West Riding that eventually the millowners in Halifax and district protested as a body at the way in which Baker was implementing the Act.

After twenty-four years of strenuous prosecution Baker was appointed Inspector for the Midland district in 1858. His move there was eventually to bring him into contact with Smith. In 1863 he paid a routine visit to the

Whitwick Colliery Company and the two met. It was not only a meeting of minds; it was the meeting of twin souls. They were both men of passionate conviction, their views vigorously expressed in speech and writing. Both men were frequently too outspoken for their own good or for that of their causes and as a result made enemies only too easily. Both were Liberals, driven by a reforming zeal, determined to improve the condition of the labouring poor and especially that of their children. Both also recognised the vital role of education in improving the lot of the children and were ahead of their time in advocating a unified system of education with qualified and trained teachers. The two men found their views and hopes identical and the visit signalled the start of a life-long friendship.

Baker, a vastly experienced inspector who had seen many distressing situations during his career, was shocked by Smith's revelations of the physical and moral squalor in the brick-fields and soon shared Smith's concern over the plight of the children there. He sought his help in presenting his section of the *Reports of the Inspectors of Factories to Her Majesty's Principal Secretary of State for the Home Department* in 1864. Smith's influence is very apparent in the Report to which Baker added a gloss of his own:

> I have seen a boy of five years old working among two or three-and-twenty females being 'broken in', as they call it, to the labour. I have also seen females of all ages, nineteen or twenty together, indistinguishable from men, except by the occasional peeping out of an earring, sparsely clad, up to the bare knees in clay splashes, and evidently without a vestige of womanly delicacy, thus employed, until it makes one feel for the honour of the country that there should be such a condition of human labour existing in it.

In the course of his investigations Baker found that although a number of four-year old children were found working in the brickfields, these were happily the exception. He was still confronted, however, with the unpalatable fact that the usual age at which this child-labour began was, for girls as well as boys, from seven to eight years.

"How, in the name of humanity, is it possible," exclaimed George Smith, in commenting on the report, "to get manly men or womanly women physically out of creatures from whom the maximum of toil is exacted with the minimum of strength and of recompense? Labour, brow-sweat, hard-earnings, come soon enough without being thus anticipated and hastened, and without having God's august gift of life stunted, crushed, contorted, in its first outgrowth.... It is tampering with the very seedcorn of the great afterharvest of our national life."

Yet, as Baker knew to his cost, a thorny path lay ahead of them. The movement to reform the abuses of child labour, especially the grotesque length of their working day, had been slow to get under way and had built up little momentum. The reformers were unusual bed-fellows. They included a number of humane manufacturers (there were some), churchmen of various denominations, with Evangelical Christians prominent among them, and, rather surprisingly, many Tory landowners plus the Tory press. This alliance cut right across normal party lines. All were agreed that something should be done to alleviate the distress of the children but they found it hard to bring in effective legislation in the teeth of opposition from the manufacturers. Progress in attempting to regulate the working conditions and the hours of labour of women and children was scandalously slow, criminally so in the view of Hutchins and Harrison, our authority on factory legislation. One historian acidly observed that it took twenty-five years of legislation to restrict a child of nine to a sixty-nine hours week, and that only in cotton mills.

The employers, bred to a tradition of an inexhaustible supply of cheap labour, were strongly opposed to interference in their concerns by either humanitarians or parliamentarians. They viewed any such action as an attack on capital and private property, both regarded as sacrosanct in the high-noon of laissez-faire. From the beginning of the century the legislation promoted by Sir Robert Peel (1750–1830) and Lord Shaftesbury (1801–1885) had been primarily aimed at improving conditions in the textile industries. This left the rest of industry wholly unregulated and untouched by reform. The 1833 Factory Act, the Ten Hours Bill of 1847, which was the culmination of the struggle led by Richard Oastler and Michael Sadler, and other minor Acts designed to limit the hours of labour of children and women, all still applied mainly to the textile trades. This situation could not continue indefinitely. Although it took some years and much agitation, it was gradually borne upon interested members of Parliament that even if conditions in the textile mills had been appalling, those in other industries were just as bad, if not worse in some respects, and should be similarly brought under control.

Spurred on by the reports of the Third Commission on Children's Employment, set up by Shaftesbury in 1861, six trades as diverse as pottery and hosiery were brought under the regulations of existing factory legislation by the Act of 1864. Further reports on a whole range of industries, ranging from iron shipbuilding to artificial flower and feather making and from india-rubber works to brick-fields (Baker's contribution) revealed that shocking conditions were common throughout the whole spectrum of manufacturing and were generally worse in smaller work places than in larger ones. This led inexorably to the conclusion that the areas of industry not currently covered should be brought under the umbrella of the Factory Acts forthwith.

In March 1867 the Government introduced a Factory Acts Extension Bill and at the same time a Bill for the regulation of workshops. The former assumed that all work places, large and small, could not be dealt with uniformly so it was decided, despite some dissenting voices, to distinguish the larger from the smaller establishments by the number of people employed in them. The figure was set quite arbitrarily at fifty; this being, one presumes, either twice twenty five or half one hundred! The Factory Acts Extension Act brought all premises in which fifty or more people were employed in a manufacturing process within the scope of factory law. Such factories were thus liable to inspection by government inspectors. In its turn the Workshops Regulation Act brought under control all premises employing fewer than fifty persons and these became the responsibility of the local authorities.

Under the main provisions of the Workshops Act no child under eight could be employed in any handicraft; children from eight to thirteen might only be employed under the half-time system, whereby they had to attend school for a minimum of ten hours a week, instead of three hours a day or on alternate days, as in factories. Young persons and women might only be employed for twelve hours, less one and a half hours for meals. Though the working hours were restricted to the same number as those under the Factory Act, the limits within which these hours might be taken were much wider. Children might work between 6a.m. and 8p.m., young persons and women between 5a.m. and 9p.m. but this swiftly led to abuses. The solution could only be the establishment of a 'normal day', namely a fixed period of employment equal to the number of working hours permitted plus meal times, but that was some years off.

I have dealt with this latter Act in some detail because of its importance in our story. Smith and Baker were concerned that, although the large Brick and Tile Yards were placed under the mandatory Factory Acts, the Workshops Regulation Act governing the smaller yards was only a permissive measure. Its provisions were at the mercy of the local authorities who could determine the extent to which they would enforce them. In the event a few did so, some flatly refused to do so, while the majority ignored the Act. Thus the small brick-yards employing less than fifty hands continued as before without hindrance, happy to ignore the conditions and abuses that had outraged Smith for so many years.

The Act proved particularly difficult to administer. Situations arose where two brick-yards doing much the same work but on a different scale were operating next to each other. One was strictly governed by the Factory Acts while the other fell under a quite different and poorly-drafted set of regulations. The result, as might be expected, was confusion among the inspectors and bad blood between competing employers. It is hardly surprising the Act became virtually a dead letter.

Eventually a Commission was set up in 1867 to examine the whole body of factory law with a view to its consolidation. The Commission recommended the repeal of the Factory Acts of 1864 and 1867 plus the Workshop Regulation Act of 1867, and in the fullness of time a consolidating Factories and Workshop Act was passed in 1878. This Act simply abolished the distinction between factories and workshops as places where either more or less than fifty persons were employed — a sensible reform for which Smith had long argued. The distinction was now to be the use or non-use of mechanical power. A work place using mechanical power was a factory; a work place not using mechanical power was a workshop. One has to admire the elegance of this solution.

A Picture

I saw a little brick-yard boy
With body almost bare,
What clothes he had were thin and torn,
And matted was his hair;
And such a little boy was he,
In years, not more than three times three.

And yet for very little pay
He'd work so hard the live long day;
From six at morn, till seven or eight,
His legs had tumbled 'neath the weight
Of forty pounds of clay or more,
And ah, poor lad! his feet were sore.

No wonder, either, for those feet
A many miles had run,
With hurried speed across the floors,
Beneath a burning sun;
No wonder at his silent tears,
His master's oaths rung in his ears.

And he could neither read or write,
Nor tell his A B C;
And he but little knew of God,
Who made the earth and sea;
Poor little slave on British soil,
So young in years, why dost thou toil?

Methinks that thou should'st go to school,
Till thou art stronger grown,
And learn to read, and count, and write,
Before thou leav'st thy home,
To labour here so hard and long;
Ah! stay, poor child, till thou art strong.

I wish I could, but father drinks,
And beats poor mother so,
And then he swears at me and says
That I to work shall go.
I wish sometimes that I were dead,
Only poor mother has no bread.

Poor child, said I, and turned my head,
To hide the starting tears,
God send a friend that will protect
Thy young and tender years,
And thousands more as young as thee,
From drink's dead curse and slavery.

Anon

Chapter 5: The Dream

"I make no pretence at fine sentence-writing. I aim at telling simply a dark chapter in 'the annals of the poor'. Throughout I speak that I do know."

George Smith: *The Cry of the Children*

The stress of their first few years at Coalville, stemming from the hostile atmosphere both at the works and in the Sunday School, had taken their toll on Mary. Their living conditions, her recent poor health and worry over her children contributed to her decline and she began to fail. Early in 1866 her condition worsened and on 19th January she died in Smith's arms; she was only thirty-seven. Mary was buried in Coalville churchyard and Smith describes the dismal scene: "It was a very dark, cold slushy day, and deep snow lay on the ground with large flakes falling upon us as I and four motherless little ones followed her to the grave which was partly filled with snow, water and clay — a puddle hole — into which she was lowered, never to see her again." The inscription on her grave read as follows:

Her life was peaceful
Her death triumphant
In
Affectionate Remembrance of
Mary
The Wife of George Smith
She was born at Tunstall
On the 12th of March 1828
and died at Coalville
on 19th January 1866

Given the problems at his works, and now with small children to look after as well as an ageing father, Smith was in an unenviable position, He was not to remain so long. Being a determined man and one who saw some matters with a disarming clarity, Smith set about solving his problem. Idealist and dreamer he might be, but Smith was a practical man where his domestic happiness was concerned. Exactly two months later, on 19th March, he married Mary Ann Lehman, aged thirty-two, daughter of a framework knitter. His second Mary had been a Church of England Sunday School teacher for fifteen years in the village of Ockbrook in Derbyshire. If there seems a touch of the funeral baked meats about this union, it should be remembered that such brief intervals between marriages were not uncommon in Victorian England.

His second marriage was to be as successful as his first. Mary, besides providing a loving mother for his children, proved a supportive wife, flinging herself enthusiastically into Smith's various activities, particularly the evangelical and Sunday School side. With Mary's help, he steadily developed his Sunday School, trebling its numbers and extending its services. Smith himself took two services regularly each Sunday as well as attending many meetings in Coalville, London and elsewhere in connection with the Primitive Methodist movement. He and Mary also laid the foundation stones of several chapels and Sunday Schools in the district and helped to raise funds for the buildings.

His financial position, too, was also improving. He had enjoyed several small annual rises in salary since he was first employed by the Whitwick Colliery Company as manager. Now his strenuous efforts on their behalf began to be better rewarded and in 1867 his salary was raised to two hundred pounds per annum. About this time he began to take an active part in local politics in the Liberal cause, seeing this as a natural step along the pathway to his goal of brick-yard reform. His political activities lasted until 1874 and it will be more convenient to deal with these in a later chapter. It should be remembered, however, that the political contacts he made were to prove of vital importance in his campaign to improve the conditions of the children in the brick-yards.

The following year, 1868, was to be a significant one for Smith. It started promisingly with the birth of a daughter, Clara Lehman, on 21st. January. His business affairs, like his Sunday School work, continued to prosper. He had considerably increased his workforce in his yards at Coalville and Ibstock and he now had a staff of 65 men, plus 63 boys aged over 12, 35 of whom were over 13. No women or girls were employed. He had so influenced and encouraged his men that of the sixty-five he could claim twenty Primitive Methodists, two Wesleyan and two Baptists. Among this number were eight local preachers, five class leaders and three Sunday School Superintendents.

He had also proved, much to the irritation of manufacturers in the district, that reducing the hours of labour for young children did not result in lower production. Like a few far-sighted others, he found from experience that during the last hour or two of the day fatigue caused carelessness and a much reduced output that not even blows or oaths could correct. He continued to maintain there was little sense in employing children aged seven to ten, when boys of eleven to thirteen were able to do twice as much work, even though their wages were a little higher.

He was still engaged in a somewhat desultory correspondence over the plight of the brick-yard children but during the spring he began to feel he was at last in a position to take up the cause he had held dear for some years. Although the Workshops Act was now in place, we have seen that it had made virtually no impact on the industry. The smaller brick-yards, run by what Smith called "high-handed and slippery evaders of every claim of humanity", had little to fear from the local authorities. As for the large yards, they received only a very occasional visit since the few factory inspectors had such extensive areas to police and so many factories within their jurisdiction. Thus bad conditions and ill-usage in many works went on unknown and unchecked. Smith felt strongly that if progress was to be made then a forceful campaign was needed to stamp out the exploitation of child labour in the industry as a whole by bringing the smaller yards under the control of the Factory Acts. This would make them subject to regular inspection and enforcement. It is difficult to estimate with any accuracy the number of children and young girls aged between four and sixteen working in the brick-yards but the figure might be as high as twenty-five thousand.

In the summer he wrote to Robert Baker and told him that he had determined to campaign whole-heartedly on behalf of the brick-yard children. He admitted that his efforts during the earlier years of the decade had been spasmodic and unco-ordinated; he had written some letters but these had been mainly addressed to private individuals. Now he had decided to bend all his considerable energies of tongue and pen to the cause.

Throughout his life Smith was highly susceptible to the influence of dreams, inordinately so at times. These he could remember and relate in stupefying detail. For many years his daily diary entry began with a record of his dreams the previous night: terrifying, elaborate, grotesque, fanciful or solemn. If his dreams occasionally involved Queen Victoria and members of the Peerage, this is only a reflection of the part he assumed them all to be playing during his campaigns. He tells (and I promise I shall only quote this one example) how one night in the summer of 1868:

> I dreamt that I was going up an exceeding high mountain, and as I was starting from the base of it to get to the summit, thousands of poor little ragged, half-naked brick-yard children, of both sexes, clustered round me, with tears in their eyes, and with looks and cries that pierced my innermost soul, which I cannot and shall not attempt to erase from my memory— 'Master, pull me up! Master, pull me up!' Some of the children would lay hold of my coat, others I would take by the hand, and in this way I toiled up the mountain till near the top; and just as I was about to give up the struggle, the Prime Minister appeared upon the scene. We both now began to pull the poor things up to the top, but were not strong enough for the task — a labour of love — and just as we were about to give up the struggle, our good and noble Queen came to the rescue, and the result was we finally landed them upon the top. Taking off my hat, I shouted at the top of my voice, 'Hurrah! hurrah! We've won! we've won!' to such a degree that I woke my wife with my shouting. I was in a great state of perspiration, and she was afraid I was 'gone beside myself'. Strange to say, this state of things happened three nights in succession.

Not only did Smith have this dream three nights running, he also had it rather conveniently several years later just as he was thinking about embarking on a crusade on behalf of the canal children. The details were slightly different but the Queen and her Prime Minister again appeared and he took it as a spur from on high to take up the challenge.

It may have been only a dream but it had a dramatic effect on Smith. He immediately wrote his first letter to the press, published by *The Morning Star* on 26th July, to be followed in the course of years by literally thousands of others. Smith was to become one of the nineteenth century's most prolific letter writers and propagandists. We find an example of his letter-writing feats recorded in his diary entry for 28th January, 1894, when he was already over sixty and in poor health:

> January 28: I sent seventy-eight letters to the leading press in the country, which will do much good in preparing the way for my Bill, I was 'done-up' after the work.

His letter to the editor ran as follows:

> Sir — Having had the management of extensive colliery works for many years, I can testify to the truth of the statement made by Mr. Mundella, M.P. in the House of Commons last week in the debate on the

Trades Union Bill, that 'there was no trade in which ignorance, vice and immorality prevailed to a greater extent than amongst the employees in brick and tile yards.' What is the reason? The answer will be found in the fact that children of both sexes are put to work at the most tender age, sometimes as early as six, and employed on an average fourteen and fifteen hours a day (in addition to several hours on the Sabbath), nearly naked, without any kind of supervision or separation of the sexes. Can it, then, be wondered at 'that ignorance, vice, and immorality prevail' to a greater extent in this than any other trade?

The custom prevails in many districts where children are allowed to run wild in the streets until strong enough to carry a lump of clay or a couple of bricks, and then are packed off to the yards to undergo excessive toil and, were it not for the counteracting agency of Sabbath-schools, left to grow in the grossest ignorance. If agricultural gangs and other trades are brought under the Factory Act, why not brick-yards, irrespective of the number employed in them? Manufacturers who employ fifty hands are under its restrictions whilst those who employ less escape, thereby giving them an advantage over the larger firms, at the expense of the morals of the employed. What I contend for is the application of the Act to all yards, regardless of the number of hands employed — on the ground that what is good for fifty children must be beneficial for twenty or a less number.

In the interest of the young people employed, I would appeal to the masters whose yards do not come under the Act to bring about a better state of things by voluntarily submitting them to its provisions, and thus wipe away, as soon as possible, the stigma now attached to the trade. If this is not responded to, then I ask that the Act be modified so as to bring within its beneficient protection the rising generation of the poor.

Having delivered this opening shot, Smith stood back and braced himself for an avalanche of correspondence from all parts of the country. Like so many men of strong convictions and burning sympathies, he could not bring himself to believe that others could be indifferent or opposed to such a cause. He waited and he continued to wait. To his surprise and chagrin, there was no response to his letter. Undeterred, Smith launched out on a letter-writing marathon to the provincial and national press. In subsequent letters he fulminated against the treatment of the brick-yard children: the long hours of arduous labour, the employment of very young children of both sexes and their exposure to coarseness and vice of the grossest kind.

The months passed and there was still little response. Finally, Smith decided in November 1869 to write to *The Times* in an attempt to harness the goodwill of its readers. He had now broadened his approach to include much more emphasis on the need for the children to be given better opportunities for education. A modicum of school attendance was already a compulsory condition for employing children in industry, but evasion by manufacturers and parents was widespread. This was especially true of the small unregulated brick-yards. He was convinced that *The Times* would be willing to take up such a worthy and urgent cause as "the newspaper of the civilised world". Supreme the 'Thunderer' might be, but its editor was not impressed and he told Smith that his letter could only appear as an advertisement for which the charge would be £5. Smith was outraged by this decision on a matter of public concern ("a black-burning shame" he called it) but he decided to pay the money and the 'advertisement' duly appeared.

In his letter Smith raised the problems of the half-time system, introduced by Graham's Factory Act of 1844, under which children worked either morning or afternoon and went to school for the other part of the day. He stressed the practical difficulties of applying the half-time principle to children in the brick-yards where the system was unpopular with both employers and parents. The former did not care to be held responsible for the education of their child-employees while the latter felt there was no advantage in it for them if they had to pay for their children's schooling as well as having to forego half their miserable weekly wage. Instead, Smith wanted no child to start working before the age of twelve, and even then having to produce a certificate to show he or she had been at a day-school for at least three years between the ages of seven and twelve.

The editor of *The Times* had miscalculated. The press were uniformly hostile to his attitude and showed their resentment by printing Smith's letter in their columns without charge. It gave rise to a considerable correspondence sympathetic to Smith's cause and had the effect of drawing his name and campaign to the notice of the public. His letter also elicited a reply from Alexander Redgrave, the other Chief Factory Inspector and colleague of Robert Baker. Although he disagreed with Smith over the half-time question, he supported him in his desire to see the employment of children under twelve ended and he agreed that local authorities had been lax in enforcing the Workshops Act. Redgrave and Smith recognised that they shared similar concerns though not, perhaps, similar remedies. They now began a correspondence during which their views gradually became as one on the need for better educational provision and for young children under twelve to be excluded from the work-force in the brick-yards. Their correspondence was extensively copied by the provincial press, particularly by those newspapers covering the brick and tile counties.

There was a curious sequel to this incident. A year and a half later Smith was working in his lodgings in Great Russell Street when a messenger from *The Times* arrived bearing a letter from the manager. It stated that the editor had acted incorrectly in inserting the letter as an advertisement and Smith was therefore entitled to have his money back. He returned Smith's £5 and from that time onward *The Times* was to prove helpful in his campaigns.

Towards the end of the year Smith was affected by two sudden and unexpected deaths. First, 'Catchimquick', the principal proprietor of the Whitwick Colliery Company and by now a firm friend of Smith's, became seriously ill and died shortly afterwards. The other partners, who were well aware of Smith's value as a manager, sent for him and told him it was their wish he should continue to manage the works. There would also be no objection to him carrying on his work on behalf of the brick-yard children. At the same time they raised his salary and emoluments to the dizzy heights of £750 per annum.

This splendid news seemed to promise security for Smith and his growing family but it was tempered by the death on 29th December of his youngest son, Hollins Capper, aged five. He was buried with his mother:

> We buried him in a grave in a cold, cheerless wet cemetery, with not a flower to be seen on earth. The sad ceremony took place in the midst of deep snow, with large flakes of cloud feathers falling gently upon us. We wended our way lingeringly, sorrowfully and tearfully home to grapple with more affliction and sorrow.

On the strength of his new salary Smith was able to buy Springfield House (now demolished) which had been 'Catchimquick's' old home, and he and his family moved in soon after his son's funeral. Smith was obviously rising in the world. The purchase of Springfield House at the age of 37 marked him out as a successful man of business: he found his new status "a delightful and soul-inspiring change". His imposing new property "stood back from the road with a lodge entrance, approached by a carriage drive with luscious wall and other fruits hanging temptingly in the distance. There was an avenue of fine trees in the green sward before the house which formed a shelter for us." His spacious house enabled him to entertain a succession of important visitors connected with his brick-yard campaign and his political work. Springfield House also became an open house for ministers and local preachers on the Primitive Methodist Circuit, both on Sundays and weekdays. Smith comments that his "horse and carriage and coachman" (sic!) were at their disposal at all times to take them to their appointments.

Later in the year the Smiths' pleasure in their new-found prosperity and handsome house was crowned by the birth of another daughter, Beatrice. This went some way to compensate them for the loss of their young son a few months earlier.

Although Smith had found London and provincial editors sympathetic to his cause, the spark that would ignite his campaign was still missing. His letters to the papers and periodicals had actually produced little tangible so far, except for expressions of appreciation and encouragement, while his efforts to interest members of the Cabinet or senior officials in his cause had elicited nothing beyond polite acknowledgment of his letters. As we shall see, however, it appears that his letters did arouse the interest of one newly-elected MP, Anthony Mundella. In Mundella, Smith was to find a kindred spirit, one whose views had also been coloured by poverty and child-labour. Mundella had left school at the age of nine to help support his family and two years later he was apprenticed to a hosiery manufacturer in Nottingham. Through his own efforts he rose to become a partner and then took an active part in local politics. He had entered Parliament as a Liberal in November 1868 as the member for Sheffield, a city he was to serve with great distinction until his death in 1897. Passionately concerned with promoting the welfare of the working classes through education and factory reform, he swiftly made his mark in the new administration. Courteous but tenacious, he soon exercised considerable influence in government circles through his practical grasp of commercial problems.

Civil Service gossip intimated that this genuine and unpretentious man was ill-equipped for office, and cynics regarded him as an indecisive pulpit-cushion thumper and nothing more. But Mundella was very much more than that. Although now virtually forgotten, he deserves to be warmly remembered for his work in educational reform at all levels and for the major part he played in promoting Forster's Education Act of 1870 and the Compulsory Education Act of 1881. He was to prove a powerful friend to Smith and he helped him considerably in introducing legislation and piloting it through Parliament.

Chapter 6: The Dream Realised

> One who never turned his back but marched breast forward,
> Never doubted clouds would break,
> Never dreamed, though right were worsted, wrong would triumph.
>
> Browning: Asolando (Epilogue)

Smith now pondered his next move. After discussing matters with one or two friends, he eventually decided to draw the plight of the brick-yard children to the attention of the National Association for the Promotion of Social Science. This body was formed in 1857 with the object of furthering the development of Social Science. The Association had four departments: Jurisprudence and Amendment of the Law, Education, Health, and Economy and Trade. Annual meetings, or congresses, were held in late September and early October in large cities in England and Scotland. These meetings lasted a week and each department met separately to hear papers on contemporary social problems. Its proceedings were widely reported and the Association proved highly influential in Victorian reforming circles until its demise in 1884. Among the presidents of the Association were such luminaries as the Earl of Shaftesbury, Lords Aberdare, Brougham and John Russell, and the Lord Bishop of Manchester. Smith sought an invitation to the Congress to be held in the autumn of 1870 at Newcastle-on-Tyne to read a paper dauntingly entitled, 'The Employment of Children in Brick and Tile Making considered in Relation to the Factory and Workshops Acts'. As it turned out, this was an inspired move on his part and was to achieve results far beyond his expectations.

Smith duly arrived at the Congress where his entrance caused a minor sensation. He intrigued his audience by coming into the hall carrying an old fish-basket which he deposited at his feet on the platform. Having been introduced, he smiled benignly upon his hearers and began by telling them stories about his labours as a small boy in Peake's Tileries. He had already proved an excellent Sunday School teacher and an effective preacher, enlivening his speeches and his preaching with a quite unaffected use of the homely expressions and metaphors of his Potteries upbringing. He never lost this agreeable habit and it added a pungency and a piquancy to his addresses. Soon his Newcastle audience had fallen under his spell. Then Smith suddenly surprised them by reaching down for his fish basket and tipping out onto the table a large lump of damp clay. He declared to his listeners, who were probably wondering what this heavily-whiskered eccentric would do next:

> As a further proof of the severe and extremely heavy nature of the toil undergone by children, I would submit to your inspection a lump of solid clay weighing forty-three pounds. This, in a wet state, was taken a few days ago from the head of a child of nine years of age, who had to walk a distance of twelve and a half miles, half that distance being traversed while carrying this heavy burden.

He followed this with another poignant example:

> I had a child weighed very recently, and although he was somewhat over eight years of age, he weighed about 52 lb. and was employed carrying a 43 lb. weight of clay on his head an average distance of 15 miles daily. He worked 73 hours a week.

Smith denounced the life of ignorance and vice to which the children, especially the young girls, were condemned in the brick-yards and made an impassioned plea for action. He ended by putting forward some ideas that he would later refine into proposals for legislation. Smith was loudly applauded. His sincerity, good sense and compassion, springing from his experiences in the brick-yards, won over his audience as they were eventually to win over members of both Houses of Parliament and other influential reformers. More importantly, his address appeared in full in most of the London and provincial papers and created something of a sensation. It attracted such headlines and copy as this from the *Builders News* of 14th October:

> THE SLAVE CHILDREN OF THE MIDLAND COUNTIES.
> Wanted, several hundred children, of seven years of age, to carry five and a half tons of clay per day for sixpence....

He admitted later that "My nibbling and barking, up to this date, at the monster of sin and iniquity had hardly done more than lift up one of his eyelids." But for the moment, Smith's paper had aroused public concern.

Smith had actually chosen a propitious moment to begin his campaign in earnest. Later in the year Gladstone was to become Prime Minister at the age

The Earl of Shaftesbury

of fifty-nine for the first of his four ministries. Gladstone was a deeply religious and serious-minded leader whose moral fervour and powerful oratory had carried him to the head of his party and had captured the hearts and minds of his followers in the country. The great champion of Liberalism, known for years as 'The People's William', was now able to give full rein to his reforming zeal. He personified the new spirit that was abroad, a sea-change in the public mood, manifested in a determination to address pressing social problems and improve the lot of the working classes.

Yet Smith's paper was not universally applauded. He incurred the wrath of a number of brick-yard owners in Staffordshire, who hastily formed the Brick-yard Masters Association to protect their interests and to oppose any hostile legislation. Smith's proposed reforms also found little favour with the workers' representatives in the area who had their own reasons for avoiding regulation in the brick-yards. He was paying the price for attacking in public the vested interests of a group of influential manufacturers. The most vocal of these and the leader of a concerted attack upon him was none other than John Nash Peake, the son of the owner of Peake's Tileries for whom Smith had worked in Tunstall.

It is ironic that hostility should have manifested itself in Tunstall; as far as one can judge, apart from Peake and several of his fellow manufacturers in North Staffordshire, there was little reaction from the brick-yard owners in other parts of the country. Perhaps it was the fact that Smith had been one of his workmen that piqued Peake as much as Smith's strictures about conditions in the brick-yards. Certainly Peake was incensed by Smith's "wildest and most reckless assertions" in his address about the treatment and long hours worked by very young children and the immorality among the brick-yard workers, particularly the young women. He chose to take Smith's criticisms personally as owner of the yards in Tunstall which Smith knew so intimately.

At the end of October Peake fired off a letter to the *Staffordshire Sentinel* which was the opening shot in a vitriolic correspondence. The *Staffordshire Sentinel* was a weekly paper of high quality which, with its detailed coverage of home and European affairs, appears considerably superior to any comparable provincial weekly today. From Peake's first letter until his last in January 1871, a total of twenty-five letters arrived on the editor's desk from Peake, Smith and their various allies. While detailed reports of the Franco-Prussian War occupied the main pages, for two months the correspondence columns were filled with claim and counter-claim. I do not wish to weary the reader with a blow-by-blow account of the specious arguments, the arcane quibbles and the misleading and conflicting statistics over procedures in the brick-yards, which were paraded, inspected and dismissed by both sides.

Briefly, Peake rejected out of hand what he saw as Smith's slurs upon his workforce and the conditions in his yards. In this he was supported by some eight letters from workmen in his employ (described by Smith as "a parcel of blockheads led by a cypher"), who strongly opposed the charges of immorality and ill-treatment of the children. Their cogent letters are either a tribute to a surprising education or an indication that Peake put them up to it and gave them a helping hand. Peake demonstrated a grasp of argument, a humorous sarcasm and a command of invective that one has to admire. He attacked Smith for his inaccurate and unsubstantiated assertions and demanded he produce chapter and verse. Smith retorted that he stood by what he said at Newcastle-on-Tyne and further touched Peake on the raw by stating he proposed "to confirm all from Mr. Peake's own Tileries and similar". He promised that he would supply further details and evidence in a book he was writing. One cannot help having a sneaking sympathy for Peake, even though he was more than capable of looking after himself. Some idea of the tone and language of Smith's letters can be gauged by his description of the controversy;

> Mr. Peake chose to apply every 'jot and tittle' of my statement to his works exclusively and allowed himself such licence of vituperation (culminating in a blustering announcement of legal proceedings that served only to make him supremely ridiculous from the brave words of the first announcement, and the poltroonly backing out on the proverbial second thoughts) as the most furious street-rowdy or renowned Biddy herself could not hope to emulate.... A "Master', a 'gentleman' (ahem!) so immaculate as the great John Nash Peake, Esq. never could allow the 'respectability' of his Works to be impugned, never! and so the choler rose and rose, and the humble writer was to be crushed beneath the avalanche of the would-be big man's wrath.

And there is much more of this in the same vein. Peake responded rather amusingly by comparing Smith to Luke Honeythunder in Dicken's *Edwin Drood*, who was accused of calling out to his fellow creatures, "Curse your souls and bodies, come here and be blessed." Peake claimed that Smith's philanthropy was, like Honeythunder's, "of that gunpowderous sort that the difference between it and animosity was hard to determine."

Towards the end of December the correspondence took a new turn. The editor finally lost patience with this tedious exchange and ruled that in future any letters had to be inserted as advertisements — at a cost. The letters dried up. Smith, who was getting the worst of the argument and had had enough of advertisements since his recent clash with *The Times*, refused to carry on what was proving an expensive and nugatory exercise. After one last long blast Peake followed suit. A blessed calm descended upon *The Sentinel*.

Smith was now busy with his book about the brick-yards while Peake was preparing to bring out a pamphlet of his own. This was published in the spring of 1871 and was entitled *Brick-yard Children: an answer to the charges of Mr. George Smith against 'The Tileries', Tunstall*. Peake's declared aim was "the vindication of the character of a large body of workpeople who had been most wantonly, cruelly and unjustifiably attacked and vilified." His pamphlet is basically a re-working in typically trenchant style of the arguments of his letters.

In fairness Peake's pamphlet cannot be dismissed out of hand. It is, as far as we know, the only consistent challenge to what were seen by some owners as Smith's emotive and extravagant slurs upon their industry. Despite Peake's self-righteousness and refusal to accept any kind of criticism, it does seem that Smith in his disturbing pictures of brick-yard conditions may have over-egged the pudding in his efforts to arouse the public to the plight of the children. One does not doubt the hardships Smith suffered and the moral squalor he observed in his youth, but the reality, even in Peake's yards, was surely not quite as uniformly black as Smith painted. The rebuttal of his charges by the brick-yard workers themselves bears witness to this, even allowing for their wish to be seen supporting their employer. Elements of ill-usage and appalling conditions were to be found in all brick-works of the time.

Back in Coalville, Smith's sudden burst of fame and prosperity had its end in its beginning. His success in business and with his Sunday School, and now with his name appearing prominently in the press, triggered off a wave of animosity, envy and resentment against him. Coalville obviously felt that Smith was getting too big for his boots. He lacked neither courage nor determination but tact had never been his strong suit in dealing with those who resisted reform either in the brick-fields or among the Nonconformists. During his years in Coalville he had made numerous enemies among the manufacturers in the district with his refusal to employ women and young children in the large brick-yards he managed. The fact that, under his management, the profits at his works were growing considerably more rapidly than elsewhere only served to increase the jealousy. He particularly inflamed local opinion in the course of his campaign in the papers by styling himself 'George Smith of Coalville'. This suggested a certain arrogance, although Smith protested later that his territorial title had been given to him "by public acclamation and by his friends in the press and by peers and MPs in Parliament". Smith was immensely proud of his title and he continued to use it until his death.

But it was the last straw as far as Coalville was concerned. Ill-feeling had been slowly building up during the last few years and now it boiled over. He wrote years later that "To drive four separate one-horse chariots and steeds, namely, the Brick-yard Children's Chariot, the Sunday School Children's Chariot, the Politician's Chariot, and the Capitalist's Chariot abreast for so long to a successful issue without a 'spill' would have taxed the tact, courage and ingenuity of a Jehu or a Togarmahian".* But this was to be no ordinary spill. Smith began to be openly insulted and occasionally threatened wherever he went in the district while Mary and the children were followed through the streets of Coalville and shouted at and abused. This public outburst culminated in Smith's effigy being burned at a stake outside his house one night by a jeering crowd to the musical accompaniment of "a cracked band". It reminds one of the skimmington-ride in Hardy's *The Mayor of Casterbridge*.

Smith stubbornly rode out this storm and completed putting the finishing touches to his book, a very slim volume entitled *The Cry of the Children from the Brick-yards of England, with Remedy*. It was published in May 1871 and addressed to H.A. Bruce, the Home Secretary. Bruce, a Liberal MP for several Welsh constituencies, was to have a distinguished career in government, including a notable contribution to education. Created Lord Aberdare in 1873, he later became the first Chancellor of the University of Wales. Some two thousand copies of *The Cry* were widely distributed to members of Parliament, the press and to various sympathisers and institutions. It should be stressed here that throughout his struggles on behalf of the brick-yard children Smith received no financial help of any kind and met the entire expenses of the campaign out of his own pocket. This included the cost of printing and distributing *The Cry of the Children*.

He took his title from a poem with the same title by Elizabeth Barrett Browning. This is a sentimental effusion that has little appeal for us today, containing such pathetic lines as:

> "True", say the children, "it may happen
> That we die before our time;
> Little Alice died last year — her grave is shapen
> Like a snowball, in the rime."

Her work was very much to the taste of her Victorian audience with its heady mixture of sentiment and religiosity. It naturally affected Smith with its reflections on the evils of child-labour:

---

*Togarmah was an ancient city in Asia Minor which supplied horses and mules to Tyre.

> For, all day, we drag our burden tiring
> Through the coal-dark underground—
> Or all day, we drive the wheels of iron
> In the factories round and round.

In a comment that is typical of his prose style when unmanned by emotion, Smith writes:

> All honour unto reverence, to Mrs. Barrett Browning, for her passionate lay of the *Cry of the Children*; scalding tears have bathed it with holier unction than apostolical hands.

The little book itself is essentially a compilation. It reprints Smith's address to the Social Science Congress at Newcastle-on-Tyne and his submissions to Robert Baker's Report and it also includes material from Elihu Burritt. The rest of the book is taken up with a confusing selection of Smith's articles and letters to the press (with an unconscionable amount of repetition), letters of support to the press from his sympathisers, and items of correspondence from Her Majesty's Inspectorate. It is not an easy read.

On 25th May, Smith plucked up courage and sent a copy to Lord Shaftesbury. He sent it with a brief covering letter (his first to Lord Shaftesbury whom he had not yet met) seeking Shaftesbury's "sympathy and aid in my humble efforts to secure the protection of Government for the protection of brick-yard children." Shaftesbury replied, equally briefly, but encouragingly: "The state of things is simply wicked, and the continuance of it without excuse." To have aroused the concern of Shaftesbury and to have enlisted the support of the most powerful social reformer in England was a tremendous coup.

Smith's pamphlet (it could hardly be called more) was warmly welcomed by the press and those well-disposed to the cause, and fuelled the agitation sparked off by his address to the Social Science Congress. Smith was not the man to criticise and condemn institutions, practices and abuses without being ready to suggest solutions stemming from his own experience. He was now quite clear in his own mind what he wanted to achieve by legislative action and he summarised his objectives as follows:

> 1. I seek absolutely to prohibit infant and child labour in brick-yards.
>
> 2. I seek absolutely to prohibit the employment of girls and women in the work of the brick-yards.
>
> 3. I seek to have it enacted that no one shall be permitted to work in brick-

yards sooner than the twelfth birthday, and then only when certified to be able to "read, write, and cipher".

4. I seek to reduce the hours of labour to a maximum of 8 to 10 hours, and to allow those aged from 12 to 14 to work only on alternate working days. This arrangement is preferable to halftime working, which has practical, though not unsurmountable, difficulties.

5. I seek to place all brick-yards, tileries and the like under an amalgamation of the Factory Act and the Workshops Act — including all employing under as well as over 50 hands.

6. I seek to have Inspectors and Sub-Inspectors appointed who know the usages of the brick-yards.

He now considered how best to proceed and decided to consult his friend and ally Robert Baker. The pair agreed to go to London to see Anthony Mundella, not only to enlist his help for the cause but to sound him out about what action the Government might take. Weighing up the evidence Smith and Baker laid before him, Mundella decided it was a matter either of a Royal Commission to enquire into the conditions of the brick-yard children or legislative action. On 4th June 1871 he informed Smith he felt there was little chance during the session of extending the Factory Acts to include the small brick-yards, but he stressed his determination to bring the matter before the House. To this end he asked Smith for further information he could use "in the interest of poor children and humanity". Smith responded immediately with another copy of his book and a deluge of relevant letters. These convinced Mundella that no formal enquiry was necessary since he now had all the information he needed to press on with a Bill bringing to an end the exploitation of children and young women in the brick-yards.

This meeting with Mundella marked the beginning of Smith's association with politicians on the larger stage. He may initially have cut something of a comical figure but those who met him were soon converted by the enthusiasm, determination and shining sincerity of this earnest man from the Midlands. Although Gladstone was a High Churchman, the product of Eton and Oxford, and Smith a Primitive Methodist, the product of a Dame school and the university of life, they were curiously alike in their tremendous energy, high seriousness, lack of humour, moral fervour and crusading zeal on behalf of the oppressed. Though Smith often listened to Gladstone in the House, it is a pity that we have no record of his reactions; it would be enlightening to read Smith upon Gladstone. Mundella was as good as his word and a few days later on June 13th, he introduced into the House of Commons a Bill entitled, "The Factories Acts (Brick and Tile Yards) Extension Bill, 1871". Although this did not give Smith all that he had hoped for, the major provision was that no female, and no child under ten years of age, could be employed in brick-fields and tileries. This was the signal for leading articles and reviews in nearly all the influential papers in the country to urge the Government to take up the cause. The illustrated papers, especially the *Graphic*, published photographs of the brick-yard children revealing affecting aspects of their labour. Public feeling ran so high as a result of this agitation that within a fortnight two Bills were in the Commons and another in the Lords dealing with the question.

Mundella had his finger upon the pulse of the House and he now felt that Parliament would be unlikely to agree to the total prohibition of female labour in the brick-yards. He put it to Smith that if he would accept sixteen as the age at which females could work in brick and tile yards and drop the 'no females' idea, then it would be made a Government measure. Smith, fearing for the future of his Bill, reluctantly agreed. Mundella arranged with Lord Shaftesbury that he should move an address to the Crown on the subject of the brick-yard children and that the Government would answer it by incorporating his Bill with theirs and so get everything through during the session.

Thus on Tuesday, 11th July Lord Shaftesbury spoke in the House of Lords. He quoted extensively from *The Cry of the Children* and added a telling passage from Robert Baker's report:

> I consider the employment of children in brick-yards absolutely cruel, and that the degradation of the female character in them is most complete. I have known parents in receipt of two, three, and four pounds a week send their children out to work at clay works for a few shillings per week, hung in rags, while the parents themselves rioted at home in luxuries and drink.

Shaftesbury had recently taken the trouble to visit a brick-field himself and what he encountered there profoundly affected him:

> I first saw, at a distance, what appeared like eight or ten pillars of clay, which, I thought, were placed there in order to indicate how deep the clay had been worked. On walking up, I found to my astonishment that these pillars were living beings. They were so like the ground on which they stood, their features so indistinguishable, their dress so besoiled and

covered with clay, their flesh so like their dress, that, until I approached and saw them move, I believed them to be products of the earth. I followed them to their work and then I saw what Elihu Burritt has so well described. I saw little children three parts naked, tottering under the weight of wet clay — some of it on their heads and some of it on their shoulders — and little girls with large masses of wet, cold and dripping clay pressed on their abdomens. They had to endure the heat of the kiln and to enter places where the heat was so fierce that I was not myself able to remain there more than two or three minutes.

Shaftesbury ended with an impassioned plea that such abominations should be swiftly ended. He was supported by Bishop Jackson of London who condemned the method of working in his diocese. Here children aged from 6 to 13 were employed by gang-masters who provided cheap labour for the head brickmakers. In summer, when the brick-yards were at their busiest, the children were employed from 5 am to 7 pm with three short intervals for meals. The Bishop also strongly opposed the employment of women in the brick-fields where the effect was "entire deterioration of the moral character".

The final speaker, Viscount Midleton, was brief and to the point. He said that he had questioned Mr. Smith very closely about some of the statements made in *The Cry* which seemed to him to be utterly monstrous and improbable. However, he had decided, like Lord Shaftesbury, that, appalling as Mr. Smith's descriptions were, he had in fact far understated the situation. Such a state of things was simply intolerable and should be remedied forthwith. Without further debate the motion for the address was carried and Shaftesbury was able to write to Smith the next day: "Thank God I carried the address last night. We shall have this year a Bill for the children in the brick-yards. Bless God for His grace on your efforts."

The Bill now proceeded on its way to the statute book with the all-important fifth clause now reading as follows:

> 5. After the first day of January, one thousand eight hundred and seventy-two, no female under the age of sixteen years, and no child under the age of ten years, shall be employed in the manufacture of bricks and tiles, not being ornamental tiles, and any female or child who is employed in contravention of this section shall be deemed to be employed in a manner contrary to the provisions of the Factory Acts 1833 to 1871, and the Workshops Acts 1867 to 1871.

It is only fair to let George Smith describe the culmination of his efforts in his own inimitable way:

> I shall never forget the 16th of August 1871 so long as there is a drop of 'the red water' in my body. While Mr Bruce, the Home Secretary was moving the third reading of the Factory and Workshops Act Amendment Bill, my blood seemed to be freezing in my veins, my hands and feet began to tingle as if they were full of 'pins and needles' and my head felt as if there were no life to it. The climax came, and I firmly believe that if I had not immediately jumped up and down to shake, stir, and move myself, I should soon have been insensible on the floor. Happily this sensation soon passed off. But when Mr. Speaker said,'The Ayes have it', it would have done me good to have shouted:
>
>> Sound the loud timbrel,
>> O'er Egypt's dark sea,
>> Jehovah hath triumphed,
>> His children are free.

Fortunately he resisted the temptation. Mundella saw Smith in the gallery and beckoned him to go down to the lobby. Here he received the "hearty congratulations, shakes of the hands, taps upon the shoulders" from the Home Secretary, Lord John Manners, and several other members of Parliament. Smith had finally carried the day, and with the help of Baker, Redgrave and his political allies, Mundella and Shaftesbury, had won his spurs as a reformer. He walked back from the House to his lodgings with a full heart, savouring his success, happy in the knowledge that in future no children or young girls would have to endure what he had seen and suffered as a boy in Tunstall.

Chapter 7: Little Local Difficulties

"We have scotch'd the snake, not killed it."
Shakespeare: *Macbeth*

The press were swift to endorse what Parliament had enacted and Smith's reputation was made. He was soon known throughout the Midlands as the 'Children's Friend', a well-deserved title and one that he would always treasure. His name was all over the papers and one or two were quite extravagant in their praise. The *Liverpool Courier* headlined its report of the debate with the cry of "A Statue for Mr. Smith" and continued, "Let us have a statue of George Smith, baked of brick-field clay by brick-field children". This prompted John Peake to step in and paint an amusing picture of "the effigy of Mr. Smith borne to the oven by emaciated little babies of three years, groaning grievously beneath the weight of so much worth".

This is all good knockabout stuff but it could not disguise the anger and bitterness felt by Peake about the passing of the Bill. He was furious at so little notice having been taken of his views during the third reading of the Bill, and he fulminated afterwards: "A more sensational debate, one so little creditable to legislation past and present, never disfigured our Parliamentary proceedings." He had written at some length to George Melly, the MP for Stoke-on-Trent, during the summer with his usual complaint that the abolition of female labour from brick and tile works would merely condemn these unfortunates to occupations physically and morally worse. His letter included an attack on Smith and an ill-judged comment on Mundella's knowledge of the brick trade. This was hardly likely to endear him to Melly who was an ardent Liberal and a Unitarian to boot. Melly was prominent in both public and commercial life in Liverpool during its heyday in the mid-nineteenth century. Deciding to enter national politics, he won a by-election in Stoke-on-Trent in February, 1868, defeating a powerful Tory opponent in Minton Campbell, a local chinaware manufacturer. Very much a child of his time, Melly held decided opinions on a variety of topics which he expressed with considerable bluntness. This characteristic, allied to a lack of tact and an aggressive manner, proved something of a handicap in Parliament. Yet he proved an active Liberal in the House and an effective constituency member, so much so that he was re-elected unopposed at the general election in November and again in 1874. A year later, however, he was forced to resign his seat for business reasons. His intimates claimed that, under his brusque words and peremptory manner, further honed by service as a major in the 4th Lancashire Artillery Volunteers, there lurked a kind and benevolent heart; others felt it needed some finding. Melly delayed replying to Peake until the beginning of November and then attempted to fob him off with a surprisingly long, unctuous and vacuous reply.

If Smith thought that the battle over the brick-yards had been won, he was to be quickly disillusioned. He may have won the war but there was to be no peace for several years. As a result of his reforming zeal and forceful advocacy, Smith had made some powerful friends in both Lords and Commons. He had also made enemies, who continued to dispute statements made in his Newcastle speech and repeated in *The Cry of the Children*. The same small group of irate manufacturers in North Staffordshire, led by Smith's old adversary, John Peake, now began to wage a guerilla campaign against the new Act. They fastened upon what they saw as a loophole in the Act and proposed to drive a coach and horses through it. The wording of the fifth clause gave them their opportunity. It stated that "no female under the age of sixteen years and no child under the age of ten years, shall be employed in the manufacture of brick and tiles, not being ornamental tiles...." The owners of the brick and tile yards reasoned that if they could prove that they, too, were in the business of making ornamental tiles, then they could claim they fell under the 'Earthenware' Act, part of the Factory Acts Extension Act of 1864, and thus continue to employ girls and children aged eight (and younger!) to their hearts' content.

They began to bombard Robert Baker with letters seeking clarification of the phrase 'ornamental tiles'. He consulted Smith on 10th Feb. 1872: "I think the Earthenware Act (1864) did not intend to point to any tile being 'ornamental' other than 'mosaic tiles', although I am aware that many ordinary tiles are used for ornamental purposes." Baker asked for an early reply and he received one the following day. I quote Smith's reply not only because of its relevance to the issue but also to demonstrate his mastery of his craft and the clarity with which he could write on occasions:

> ....'Ornamental tiles' is the term that can only be applied to mosaic, encaustic, and enamelled tiles. From their special peculiarities in manufacture, they can only be made in earthenware manufactories, or

similar works; in fact, the tiles are treated in many respects during the making, &c., as earthenware. The whole must be done under cover, and in warm, clean and dry factories or buildings. Some branches of the making are suitable for females, and that is one of the many reasons why they are called 'ornamental tiles' to distinguish them from plain tiles as described in the Act. 'Plain tiles' will include the manufacture of draining tiles, ridge tiles, roof tiles, garden tiles, quarries and others of the same class, which process is carried on at ordinary brick and tile yards; and from the heavy and dirty nature of the work is quite unsuitable for females under 17 years of age, and this is the reason why girls are prohibited to be employed on work of this kind.

'Plain tiles' are sometimes made to ornamental patterns, but the making and selling prices being about the same, they cannot by any possiblity be included in the term 'ornamental tiles' mentioned in the Act. The difference in preparing the clay, &c, for the two kinds is enough to satisfy anyone who has the least knowledge of the matter. The clay for 'ornamental tiles' has to be sifted, slipped, stained and dried. The clay for 'plain tiles', as before described, is treated in the same manner as the ordinary clay for bricks, viz., by grinding and pugging.

Baker thanked him warmly and added a comment which is interesting in the light of what happened (or, rather, did not happen) later: "I don't fear yet but the time will come when you will be invited to join our department. The country won't sit down without you." From this it is clear that Baker and senior officials at the Home Office had already discussed the possibility of using Smith's talents in overseeing the operation of the new law.

Peake led a deputation both of owners and representatives of the North Staffordshire Brick and Tile Workers Association to the Home Secretary, H.A. Bruce, to have their works re-classified as coming under the previous Act of 1864 as a result of the "very great hardships" caused to the trade by the new Act. What they meant by 'hardships', of course, was being unable to use cheap child labour and girls under 16 and having to employ and pay older boys and women in their stead. The case was powerfully put by Melly. Bruce came down on the side of Peake and his friends and confirmed that brick and tile-works like theirs would in future be treated as coming under the 1864 Act. Peake was jubilant at having won what appeared a significant victory and he and Melly received the congratulations of manufacturers and workers for securing justice for the trade.

Smith was furious that Peake had managed to pull the wool over the

Home Secretary's eyes, but for the moment could do nothing about it. He was also becoming concerned about the widespread evasions and subterfuges going on in the industry. He was not so naive as to believe that the introduction of his Act would work miracles overnight but he was still unprepared for the reaction against it in some quarters. He determined to speak out again, using as his platform the Social Science Congress to be held at Plymouth in October. In his Plymouth paper he dealt with Peake first. He knew exactly what Peake's Tileries produced and what he and his fellow manufacturers were up to.

> I state deliberately that tiles used for ordinary building and draining, roof-tiles, ridge-tiles, and ordinary quarries, building bricks, stable bricks, channel bricks, slope bricks, canted bricks, plain and ornamental white, blue, and brown bricks, garden tiles, skirting-edge tiles, and other goods of the same class wherein water, sand, iron, or coal dust is used to keep the clay from adhering to the moulds during the working, and are burnt in the ordinary round, square or oval kilns or ovens, along with ordinary common bricks, and open to the direct action of the fire, come under the provisions of the Act of 1871/72.

Smith next turned his fire upon the slip-shod fashion in which he considered the 1871 Act — his Act! — was being implemented by the inspectors. This was to be a theme he would return to many times during the next few years. To be fair to the inspectors, Smith's strictures should be seen in the light of the greatly increased burden put upon them. When the 1871 Act transferred the administration of the larger workshops from the local authorities to the Factory Inspectorate, the number of factories and workshops for which they became responsible rose from 30,000 in 1867 to 110,000. Smith complained that some of the new inspectors were hopelessly inexperienced and displayed a lamentable ignorance of what they were supposed to inspect. He suggested rather unkindly that they owed their appointment to family background or superior education. Smith wanted stout men and true who would be unlikely to become "the toadies, tools or dupes of the employers". He looked for men who knew the kind of workplaces they had to inspect, the type of men they were dealing with, and were unafraid to confront them. He also argued forcefully for an increase in the number of inspectors. Only in this way could systematic and efficient inspection be achieved and the integrity of the Act ensured. Perhaps Smith was unconsciously drawing up his own job-description! His emphasis on the over-riding need to stamp out the evils of child-labour won the hearts and minds of his audience. It was a powerful and emotional address and once more Smith sat down to great applause. Lengthy extracts from his paper appeared in the national press and in the provincial papers serving his part of the Midlands.

If Smith had enjoyed mixed fortunes during 1872, the following year was to be an improvement. In the spring Smith and his wife were summoned to a special meeting of the Social Science Association in London under the presidency of Lord Shaftesbury. Through the efforts of some of Smith's parliamentary friends a fund had been raised to signal the value of his services in his successful efforts on behalf of the children of the brick-yards. This is some indication of the esteem in which Smith was held. Lord Shaftesbury presented him with a handsomely-bound family Bible, a purse of £100 and an illuminated address. This was headed "To George Smith of Coalville, Leicestershire, the Brick-fields' Children's advocate", and ran as follows:

> .... We desire to express the admiration and gratitude felt by us for your persevering and successful exertions on behalf of the poor children employed in the brick-fields of this kingdom.... you resolved to do your best to emancipate the English child from a slavery almost as degrading as that of Asia or Africa. In bringing about this result, almost single-handed, you have succeeded in awakening the consciences of our legislators to the existence of a frightful evil, and at length you had the satisfaction of seeing this evil largely ameliorated by legislative enactment in the extension of the Factory Act to all brick-yards in the kingdom.

It bore the signatures of many of the leading reformers of the day including Lord John Manners (another Leicestershire man), Bruce, Mundella and other MPs, as well as lesser lights such as Robert Baker, T.T. Paget and Charles Kingsley. The Rev. Dr. Grosart, future author of *Hanani*, also signed it. Mary received a fine silver teapot. [The author has seen the Address which is in the possession of Smith's descendants but the silver teapot seems to have disappeared along the way.]

Smith was visibly unmanned by the unexpected generosity of his friends, and in reply re-iterated his determination to continue working on behalf of poor and ill-used children. Constant vigilance was required to ensure that the provisions of the new Act were being carried out both in letter and spirit. He asked his friends to turn their thoughts and feelings away from him and concentrate on the cause he represented, and he ended with the stirring and moving cry: "Remember the children!"

Lord Shaftesbury rounded off the proceedings by praising Smith's labours and endorsing his views on inspection and inspectors. He then added that he had hoped at one time that Smith would have become an inspector. (Cheers) "For such a position he could conceive of no man more fitted by experience. But the higher powers had over-ruled it.... Nevertheless, he hoped that the time would come when Smith would be at the head of a department in this country where he would be more thoroughly enabled to carry out his great mission." To receive such praise from Lord Shaftesbury whom Smith had idolised for years was deeply gratifying and more than compensated him for the vilification he had undergone during his campaign. Smith returned to Coalville with the plaudits of the great and the good ringing in his ears.

It would seem from Shaftesbury's remark that Smith, despite having friends in high places like Manners, Bruce and Mundella, had been blackballed by officials in the Home Secretary's department. They may have felt that the appointment of such an aggressive reformer as inspector would provoke a hostile reaction from vested interests in the industry. Again, these same vested interests may have been active behind the scenes, lobbying and bending ears. Or perhaps the Department simply considered Smith was not enough of a gentleman; he had certainly not gone to the right school. But any disappointment Smith may have felt was hardly relevant now. As a successful man of business he had no need to look for a secure administrative post.

In considering the years that followed, it should be remembered that it was in October 1873 that Smith decided to launch his second major crusade, this time on behalf of the canal children. Yet even while he was engaged on this venture, and also undertaking a new commercial project in Coalville, as well as continuing his political and Sunday School work, he was still concerned in seeing that his Brickyard Act was being enforced. It was a work-load that would have crushed lesser men. Smith was made of sterner stuff but even he, as we shall see in the next chapter, was forced into giving up certain of his activities the following year.

Meanwhile, it appeared the day was not entirely lost. Smith's Plymouth Paper, the arcane arguments over what were plain tiles and what were ornamental ones, plus Mundella's misgivings over Bruce's decision had led the Home Secretary to have second thoughts. He ordered a test case to be held before magistrates in Hanley in the heart of the Potteries. It was a good choice because the magistrates were local men with extensive knowledge of the trade and unlikely to be browbeaten or hoodwinked. Once again Peake and the North Staffordshire Brick and Tile-makers Association put forward their case but Hanley was not Whitehall. To Smith's delight and relief, they lost the day.

This was not to be the end of the matter, however. Peake, as obstinate as Smith himself and unwilling to admit defeat, continued to huff and puff against the Act, and two years later he suddenly re-surfaced. Early in 1875 he learned that the Royal Factory and Workshops Commission, which met periodically to take evidence upon the operation and effectiveness of factory legislation, was intending to sit at the Queen's Hotel in Hanley. Peake saw this as an opportunity for one last effort to reverse the decision of the Hanley magistrates. But he had once more under-estimated his wily opponent. Smith had also heard of the Commission's visit and he hastened to Hanley where he put up at the same hotel. He recalled:

> The next morning about seven o'clock I went into a builder's yard and bought a blue brick, garden tile, dust brick, 6 inch quarry, a roof tile, made of the ordinary brick clay found in the neighbourhood, and an 'ornamental tile' made at an earthenware factory, and took them into the room where the Commission would meet at nine o'clock, and placed them upon the chimney-piece.

When the Commissioners assembled after breakfast, they were greeted by a genial Smith who quickly initiated them into the difference between the two types of tile. When Peake was called before the Commission, he was subjected to an informed grilling as he tried once again to convince them that the trade would be seriously damaged unless he and his friends could return to the cosy world of the 1864 Act. Then the cat was let out of the bag. It emerged that when the 1864 Act was being put into force, Peake stated that the tiles he manufactured were not ornamental and so his works did not come under it. Yet, when the 1871 Act was introduced, he had argued that these self-same tiles were actually ornamental and that his works should therefore be once again excluded. The members of the Commission were unimpressed by his special pleading and unsympathetic to the attitudes revealed by it. They felt the Brick-yards Act of 1871 was needed in the interests of common humanity and they recommended that no change should be made to the existing law. Thus the matter was finally settled in Smith's favour. Peake was dismissed, but not before one of his associates had pointed Smith out to him and whispered, "That's Smith, that's Smith". Strange as it may seem, Peake and Smith had never actually met before; they had only indulged in vitriolic correspondence. Now Peake glared at Smith, coloured, and stalked out without a word. This was the end of the road for the brick and tile makers, masters and men, and their opposition melted away.

Later in the meeting Smith was pleased to tell the Commissioners, with some relish, that the young girls formerly employed in the brick-yards in the area had little difficulty in finding other jobs. Most of them went into service. In these surroundings, although the work was hard, they soon became alienated from the very idea of brick-making and none returned to the brick-yard when they became eligible to do so at the age of sixteen. The females now employed there were either those who had been taken on over the age of sixteen or the wives of brick-makers. Encouragingly, there were now more boys coming into the labour market to take the place of girls and there was very little Sunday work.

Smith was not the man to rest on his laurels. No sooner had he outmanoeuvred Peake than he immediately turned his attention to the slow progress made in enforcing the Act. He had not altered his view that the cause was the failure of the inspectorate to carry out their duties properly. Many brick-yards had not received a visit for years and a few inspectors were happy to turn a blind eye to the continued use of child labour. Smith was so angered by what he saw as dereliction of duty among a number of inspectors that he determined to bring this yet again to the notice of the wider public. He chose his usual platform, the next meeting of the Social Science Congress at Liverpool in 1876. He had been invited to give a paper there on the plight of the canal children as part of his campaign on their behalf. He decided instead to split his paper into two parts. The first would now highlight problems of inspecting the brick-yards while the second would deal, as arranged, with the condition of the boat children.

Some weeks before he was due to deliver his paper, Smith set out to visit brick and tile works in various parts of the country so that he could form an up-to-date picture of what progress was being made. It was a discouraging journey. Smith found to his dismay that his reputation had preceded him; young girls and children employed in some works scurried away to hide when they heard he was about, while their employers gave him the rough edge of their tongues — and in the brick-yards this could be very rough indeed. All this Smith duly retailed to his audience and he complained with some justification:

> If the Act had been properly carried out at the commencement, the difficulty — if any — would long before this have been removed. If, after the passing of the Act, the whole of the machinery had been set in motion at once by first sending a short plain circular, with an abstract of the Act with the pains and penalties attached, to each works, and then to have been followed by an inspector, whose object for the first visit or two should have been to instruct and not to prosecute.... imaginary difficulties would have been removed, and we should long before this have had the whole thing running smoothly.

This eminently sensible approach shows Smith to advantage. He was also man enough to admit that, despite his criticisms, there had been a considerable improvement over the years in conditions in the brick-yards and he paid tribute to the work of the Inspectorate. But he could not resist climbing onto his hobby-horse and tilting at those who wanted 'gentlemen' to be appointed inspectors. If 'gentlemen' made the best inspectors, why not employ them as police officers, School Board inspectors, warders etc.? What was needed, he claimed, were experienced and practical men (like Smith, for example) happy to visit brick and tile yards, collieries, iron-works and similar places, armed simply with the Queen's authority. Tough eggs only need apply.

Smith continued to be critical of the way in which the provisions of his Act were being enforced, but he was now fully engaged in his campaign on behalf of the canal children. He was always to regard the Brick-yard Act as his major work, which it certainly was. He would achieve a further success but not on the scale of the brick-yard legislation. Much as he loved children and greatly concerned as he was about the canal and travelling children, it was the boys and girls of the brick-yards that remained closest to his heart.

In the years following the passing of the Brick-yard Act, there was a series of events at Coalville, hinted at in an earlier chapter, that brought ruin and hardship upon Smith and his family. It is to these that we shall turn after we have considered his venture into local politics.

Chapter 8: The Political Animal

> Blow, blow, thou winter wind,
> Thou art not so unkind
> As man's ingratitude.
>   Shakespeare: *As You Like It*

Edwin Hodder, Smith's first and only biographer, maintains that Smith was not a political animal. This is so manifestly untrue that we can only assume that Hodder deliberately omitted Smith's involvement in Leicestershire politics, much in the same way that he left out all mention of his tempestuous years in Coalville while managing the Whitwick Colliery Company's works, in order to highlight his activities in his three major reform campaigns. Yet to bring his schemes to fruition Smith had to plunge into the twilight world of lobbying and compromise. This did not require subtle political skills on Smith's part but it did involve him in pamphleteering, preaching and persuasion which were his forte.

Like many other Midland counties, the political history of Leicestershire showed a consistent pattern across the centuries. Political activity was virtually confined to parliamentary elections when matters were amicably settled by arrangement among the leading aristocratic families. From the Civil War to the end of the nineteenth century the Dukes of Rutland at Belvoir Castle were the dominant influence and there were few occasions when a member of the Manners family was not representing a Leicestershire constituency in the Whig interest. This happy pattern was fractured by the development of industry through the expansion of stocking-frame knitting and the exploitation of the Leicestershire coalfield. Industrial villages, such as Coalville, grew quickly and gave rise to the emergence of a class of manufacturers, bankers and capitalists. Many of these men, some of modest background, tended to incline towards liberalism, free trade and nonconformity.

There was another factor, too. During the Napoleonic Wars conditions for the working classes had steadily worsened in both agriculture and industry. Wages were reduced, food-prices rose and a spirit of unrest, exemplified by the Luddite riots, permeated the country. Its effects can be seen in Charlotte Brontë's novel, *Shirley,* set in Yorkshire, in the scenes so vividly depicted in and around Hollow's Mill. There was a growing demand for Parliamentary reform and the great land-owners found it was no longer so easy to dragoon their freeholders to the polls to vote for their landlord's choice.

The great Reform Bill of 1832 gave a partial, though significant, extension of the franchise. In Leicestershire the borough of Leicester retained its traditional two seats while the county was divided into two constituencies, north and south, each now returning two members. This arrangement lasted until Gladstone's Bill of 1885. Following the Reform Act, Leicestershire continued to return four Tory members for nearly twenty years, thanks largely to the party's superior organisation. But Liberalism was on the march and the fight for political supremacy now centred on the general elections. Representation of the county was no longer the preserve of the leading families and land-owners and a determined challenge to the established order loomed ahead.

When Smith came to Coalville he wisely kept his Liberal views to himself. He was far too busy making a success of the Colliery Company's works and developing his Sunday School activities to think of taking an active part in politics. In any case the two county constituencies were solidly Tory. Yet, as in the early part of the century, within a few short years of his arrival at Coalville a desire for parliamentary reform again manifested itself. It seemed to many in and outside Parliament that because of the population explosion and the growth of industry, the franchise should be extended and certain constituencies re-drawn. In 1866, as a result of the vigorous campaign for reform led by John Bright, the Earl of Derby's government with Disraeli, its leading light at the Exchequer, contemplated legislation.

It was at this point and during the early part of 1867, with all going smoothly at the brick-works, that Smith began to turn his thoughts towards politics. An opportunity was soon to present itself. In November there was a by-election in South Leicestershire caused by the death of the sitting member, C.W. Packe. At the previous general election in 1865 the borough of Leicester had returned two Liberal members and this encouraged the Liberal party to challenge the Tory hold on South Leicestershire. Their candidate was Thomas Tertius Paget of Humberside Hall, a young Leicester banker and land-owner. Smith took a leading part in drumming- up support for Paget in what turned out to be a lively campaign. There was door-to-door canvassing in the twenty or so small towns and villages in the constituency and now that the Liberals were better organised, they caught the complacent Tories by surprise and Paget was narrowly elected.

At Westminster Disraeli now took his famous 'leap in the dark' and introduced a revised Reform Bill which he piloted through the House with great skill. The Act gave the franchise to one million voters and virtually doubled the electorate. In the counties those householders paying £12 in rates were now given the vote, while in the boroughs the franchise was given to all rate-paying householders, with a lodger's vote on a £10 qualification added to it. There was also a modest redistribution of seats. Although the large towns gained, the small boroughs still held rather more power than was justified. As a result of this widening of the franchise, there was now a body of voters so large that efficient party organisation in the constituencies became a necessity.

The new voters were almost entirely workers in the towns. Agricultural labourers and workers such as miners who lived in the villages and formed most of the population in the county constituencies remained disenfranchised. They were the victims, though that is perhaps too harsh a term, of the compromises necessary to ensure the Bill reached the Statute Book. In the counties the 'territorial oligarchy', the major land-owners and aristocrats, still continued to wield their customary political power. Even so, another step had been taken towards the goal of universal suffrage, though this would not be achieved until well into the twentieth century.

Smith now had the political bit between his teeth in earnest. He felt that the vastly increased electorate would be sympathetic to the causes he cherished. He organised a local committee, got himself made secretary and set about consolidating the Liberal vote. He concentrated on ensuring that the register of those eligible to vote was up to date. He also encouraged the workmen, labourers and miners in the district to build their own cottages with the twin objects of qualifying for the new reduced franchise and bettering their social position. Samuel Smiles would have approved of his objectives. Smith went further and, in a scheme which showed the influence of Robert Baker on his thinking, he persuaded Paget to provide funds for this purpose. Paget advanced the money for buying cottages "upon the deposit of the title deeds without legal charges at five per cent per annum". Paget kept the deeds while Smith collected the interest for him.

Their by-election loss in South Leicestershire had seriously upset the Tories. They blamed their defeat upon their own apathy and a defective register of voters; they also felt it unjust that residents in Leicester should have a vote in the county. Concerned about the resurgent Liberal organisation, they set to work to prepare for the next general election.

In February 1868, Lord Derby resigned as Prime Minister and was followed by Disraeli. But although Disraeli was in office, he was not in power, and when Gladstone raised the contentious issue of the Church in Ireland his Government was defeated. Disraeli asked the Queen to dissolve Parliament and a General Election was held in November.

Smith again swung into action on behalf of T.T. Paget, the sitting member. The meetings and canvassing in the villages took place during particularly bad weather with travel around the constituency being hampered by snow drifting across the narrow roads. Fortunately (and this is an indication of Smith's new status) he had his coachman drive his trap through the dark nights. Despite the weather, Smith organised dinners and suppers to keep the voters on their toes and he later claimed he did most of the work in bringing them to the polling stations in nearly one third of the division. During the campaign he entertained the candidate, his agent and leading Leicester Liberals (the party's central headquarters was in Leicester) to lunch at Springfield House several times. Yet Smith's efforts were in vain. Paget was opposed by Lord Curzon and by Sir Henry Halford's son-in-law, Albert Pell. As usual, many tenants were reluctant to vote openly against their landlords and after a hard-fought contest Paget lost his seat. Though disappointed at this result, Smith took heart from Gladstone's victory in the general election and the return of a Liberal government.

The extra work Smith had willingly undertaken for Paget, mainly in the evenings, had sapped his stamina (he was still fully involved with his three other main activities) and he became ill. Even someone as strong and determined as Smith eventually had to admit to being exhausted in body and spirit. The doctor advised him to go to Matlock to recuperate in a gentler climate and a less stressful atmosphere. Here Smith, resilient as ever, made a swift recovery and was soon able to resume work once more.

During the next few years Smith was very busy with his campaign on behalf of the brick-yard children, getting the Bill through Parliament and trying to ensure that the provisions of the Act were being properly implemented. But he still found time for his political work, nursing the constituency and ensuring that the registers were brought up to date ready for the next general election. The only local political event during this period of Gladstonian reform was the death two years later, in May 1870, of old Lord Howe. His son, Lord Curzon, succeeded to the title and took his seat in the

House of Lords. This necessitated another by-election in South Leicestershire. Although it was vigorously contested by Paget for the Liberals, the Tory candidate once more won by a handsome margin. Interestingly, this was the last open voting election to be held in Leicester; two years later in 1872 the ballot box was introduced and the glory days of the hustings were over.

This change was expected to reduce the influence of the landlords in the general election held early in 1874. Perhaps because of this the Liberals decided to fight both north and south constituencies; Henry Packe challenged Lord John Manners and S.W. Clowes in the north while Paget stood once more for South Leicestershire. Smith flung himself into what was to prove his last general election campaign with his usual vigour. He was again to the fore in organising Paget's schedule, arranging to bring voters to the polls, holding local committee meetings and ensuring there were spontaneous cheers as "the candidate marched on his untriumphant course in the land of clods, coals, cement, lime, yarn and socks."

This time the tide was running strongly against the Liberals. Gladstone had gone too far and too fast for the country's comfort and despite the far-reaching and successful reforms of his early years he had offended too many interests, including the Church, the Army and the brewers. His foreign policy was seen as a failure and his obsession with Ireland ("My mission is to pacify Ireland", he declared) contributed to his undoing. As a result, the Conservatives under Disraeli were swept into power on a swell of popular support with a majority of fifty. They were to remain in power for twenty-two of the next thirty years. In Leicestershire, Smith's candidate was again defeated at the polls and all four seats were taken by the Conservatives.

As the months passed, Smith slowly realised he had been carrying too heavy a burden for too long and that he needed to reduce his commitments. After three consecutive defeats for his candidate Smith's enthusiasm for being actively involved in local politics in the Liberal cause began to wane. He decided to retire from the post of secretary; it had become a tiresome task for which he considered he received insufficient thanks. Smith had still not learned the lesson (he never did) that gratitude is not a common human quality. Although still a radical at heart, it seems he began to feel that he did not mind much which party was in power as long as it supported his ideas for reform.

He also decided with a heavy heart to give up his Sunday School work. He had good grounds for doing so. His success had once more aroused jealousy locally and among a few of the leading officials on the circuit. There were petty squabbles and the usual back-biting, and Smith was not the type of man to remain silent in such a situation. Matters went from bad to worse in a most un-Christianlike fashion. Rather than continue in this unpleasant atmosphere Smith decided to relinquish his active role. It was a wrench for him to give up his all-important and much-loved Sunday School work, a major feature in his life since his youth in Tunstall. However, it must have been something of a relief to leave acrimony behind and concentrate his energies on more productive and fulfilling objectives.

He was still left with the management of a business venture we shall examine in the next chapter, his new campaign on behalf of the canal children and his struggle to ensure the proper working of his Brick-yards Act. It would hardly be surprising if Smith, who had a proper regard for his talents, did not feel that, with his philanthropic activities firmly established in the public mind, he was henceforth destined to play a larger part on the national stage. Little did he suspect what the Gods had in store for him and his family.

Chapter 9: Death, Dismissal and a Dismal Departure

> When sorrows come, they come not single spies,
> But in battalions.
>
> Shakespeare: *Hamlet*

The years immediately following his brick-yard triumph were to prove tumultuous ones for Smith. He was active in local politics for a few years and he spent much time trying to ensure the new Act was being implemented properly, while his Sunday School work for the moment continued to be fulfilling. It was, however, his business career that came to dominate his life in the immediate future. He would see his career flourish as never before and then watch it suffer disaster, not once but twice, blows that would have demoralised a lesser spirit.

The year 1872 openly brightly enough for Smith who could perhaps be forgiven for basking in the sunshine of public approval. He had been made even happier by the birth of another son, Arthur Grosart, at the end of the previous December. But the Lord giveth and the Lord taketh away and the spring was marred by a sad though not unexpected blow. His father had been ailing for some time and he was finally forced to take to his bed. There, with his harmonium by his side, William awaited the grim reaper, serene and with all his faculties unimpaired. He had not long to wait because he was wasting rapidly away with tuberculosis. On the afternoon of 18th March, feeling his end was near, he called the family around him and, in a typical Victorian death-bed scene, gave them his blessing. His grandchildren, young George aged fifteen and Charles aged thirteen, were also summoned and they stood at the foot of the bed and sang the 'Songs of Zion' to him. Smith has given us a dramatic account of his father's last moments:

> He always said that he would die 'game', that is with his face to the foe, Death, of whom he had been much afraid in his lifetime. But as he neared the conflict with the 'Old Chap', as he often called Death, his fears gave way to courage. At last about midnight he tremulously hummed 'We speak of the realms of the blest'. Then he rose right up in his bed and

looking through the window' exclaimed, 'I see the 'Old Chap' coming, but I am ready, blessed be God', and with a shout, 'Victory! Victory!' he passed away.

On a day of icy winds and thick snow he was buried in Coalville cemetery. Later on, a headstone was erected with a text he had personally selected: "His end was peace".

Now that his work on behalf of the brick-yard children had largely been accomplished, it was only natural that Smith's reforming zeal, which had proved so successful for one class of unfortunates, should be turned towards another. He did not have to look far or for very long. There was a class of children he had been acquainted with since his early days in Tunstall, the canal boat children, that demanded his attention.

The Trent and Mersey Canal sliced through the Potteries from north to south, bringing in the raw materials for industry and carrying away the products of the pits, potteries and brick-yards. This busy canal, with its barges, boatmen and their families, was part of the landscape in which Smith grew up. He was aware of its activities every day of his working life in Clayhills and Tunstall. He had seen at close quarters the kind of existence the boat-children and older girls endured and the squalid conditions under which they lived. Smith was profoundly moved by the plight of these boys and girls, illiterate, ignorant, dirty and ragged, maltreated and exposed to moral danger from early childhood. The abuses they suffered and their lot was as pitiable as that of the children of the brickyards. Few of them ever attended a day school or a Sunday School; the only school most of them knew was the school of hard knocks. Smith had never forgotten the sights he had witnessed on the towpath and in the boat-cabins; they had burnt themselves into his consciousness. With his various activities going well, he was now in a position to do something about it, and the cause was one close to his heart.

He was galvanised into action by another convenient dream, similar to the one he had about the brick-yard children but this time without Queen Victoria and the Prime Minister. He dreamed that:

> a sea of upturned, little, dirty, thin, pinched faces were before me, which had the picture of death, misery, destitution, destruction and woe stamped upon their countenances, crying, with piercing cries, 'Come and help us, come and help us,' whose cries, wails and moans seem to ring in my ears to the present day.

It was a cry that no fervent Christian reformer could ignore.

With Smith, once a decision had been taken, a plan of action swiftly followed. He knew that the tide of reform was running strongly in his favour and he determined it should be taken at the flood. He formally announced his intentions in a letter in October 1873 which was published in all the London papers and copied in many of the provincial daily and weekly papers. The course of this campaign will be dealt with in the next chapter. Here we are concerned with the effect his announcement had in Coalville.

We have already seen how in 1868 his success in business and in the Sunday School movement had aroused much local ill-feeling, aggravated by a press campaign on behalf of the brick-yard children which had angered local manufacturers. Sadly, hostilities were now to break out afresh in Coalville. The resentment felt against Smith was still fresh in people's minds and, as we have seen, the Brick and Tile manufacturers, smarting under the new Act, were doing all they could to make it inoperable. Smith's letter to the papers not only re-opened old wounds but alerted another powerful group, the Canal Companies, to a possible threat. These factors, plus frequent references in the press to his various activities inflamed local opinion against him once again. This time, however, he would not be able to ride out the storm.

One night in the late autumn he was summoned to a meeting with his employers. They did not beat about the bush. They required that in future he should give all his time to the management of the Whitwick Colliery Company and that he should give up his work for the children. They also added the petty and spiteful rider that his name should be removed forthwith from the Company's letters and billheads and that all correspondence should come direct to them. Smith was thunderstruck by these unexpected demands although, on reflection later, he slowly began to realise the scale of the envy and resentment his commercial success and ceaseless campaigning had aroused. Pulling himself together, he asked if they had any fault to find with his management of the works. The directors said they had not, but advised him to go home and consider his position. Smith spent a sleepless night. The following morning on his way to the works he happened to meet the directors. He recalls that:

> They accosted me without a 'Good morning' or a kindly grip of the hand, and said, 'Well, Mr. Smith, have you thought over what we said last night?' I said I had. "And what decision have you come to?"

Smith told them he could not give up his work for the children nor would he give them the whole of his time, but that he would meet them on the question of billheads and correspondence if they, in return, would give him a contract for twelve or fourteen years. They demurred at this, but when Smith pointed out — all this in the road outside a public house! — the success of the company under his management and the considerable profits he had made for them, they told him flatly that if he did not agree with their demands they would have to part. Smith replied that in that case they might as well part at once and bidding them good morning stalked off back home.

This is typical of Smith's impetuous and stubborn character. He did not even consider taking up his entitlement to a quarter's notice from the end of the quarter and it was some time before he could bring himself to go to the works again and then only to collect papers from his office. In the meantime the directors saw to it that he lost his horse, carriage and coachman, while Smith found he was no longer able to keep his handsome house.

Smith was now unemployed. The beginning of 1873 found him with a wife and five small children to support, soon to be six with the birth of another son, Edgar (Eddie) Capper Lehman. He hoped to find a new post which would enable him to carry on with his work for the children. This proved very difficult because owners and manufacturers in the area who might have been glad to avail themselves of his technical expertise and experience would have nothing to do with him. Like many in the industry, they believed, rightly or wrongly, that his philanthropy had affected their profits and they distrusted his enthusiasms.

He was now in desperate straits, although buoyed up by his shining faith that the Lord would support him and thus enable His work to go forward. He was not to remain so long, and we find here another instance of help coming from an unlikely quarter when his fortunes were at their lowest. Quite unexpectedly, some friends of his (as he thought) in Leicester invited him to join them as a partner in the establishment of a new works in the district, the venture Smith refers to as the "Northend Tile, Terra Cotta, Brick and Sand Company". Smith was to be managing director of the company (he was by far the best man in the area for the job) at a salary of £350 per annum with coal and horse and carriage, travelling expenses, and one half of the profits after $7^1/_2\%$ had been paid on the capital invested.

Suddenly Smith's financial problems were over. The future looked bright and secure, giving him a solid platform from which he could continue his work for the boat children. A formal agreement for fourteen years (the kind of contract Smith had unsuccessfully sought from the Whitwick Colliery

Company) was drawn up by his friends, and Smith, having implicit confidence in them, signed it "without scarcely reading it". Why Smith, as a successful business man, should sign a document of this importance without going through it carefully after his previous experiences, beggars belief. His trust in human nature and in good faith among men of business led him to overlook a clause in the agreement to the effect that if there were no profits at the end of two years, that is to say, after $7^1/2\%$ had been paid on the capital invested, the agreement would come to an end. One must admit that even if he had read this clause carefully he would have been unlikely to query it, given his circumstances and his confidence in his own ability.

But this was in the future. On the strength of his new post Smith rented a pleasant villa called Dial House in Coalville and engaged servants. Happy with his new contract Smith set to work with his usual energy and expertise. He took out a patent for a new kiln he had invented, secured supplies of clay, and started building the enterprise from scratch. Over the next year shafts were sunk, machinery installed in the new works and railway sidings constructed nearby. Then irritating delays began to hold up progress. Smith started to worry, as he struggled to finish the whole project, whether he would be able to make the required $7^1/2\%$ profit on what proved to be in all an investment of £18,000. It was, in fact, only in the last month of the two year period that he was able to operate normally and profitably, but Smith felt, given the circumstances, this would be sufficient to keep the agreement intact. To his astonishment the other partners held him strictly to the letter of his contract and told him that since the assumed profit had not been forthcoming his employment was terminated.[6]

> After I had left the Leicester offices, they sent a lawyer's clerk to me on the platform at the station, puffing and blowing, white and nervous, with a paper in his hand, which he handed to me in the crowd of passengers, and which was to the effect that the agreement was at an end.

We shall never really know why the other directors decided to treat Smith, their partner and managing director, in this legalistic fashion. Perhaps Smith had been proceeding too slowly for them — slowly and surely was his motto — and it is clear there had been arguments over the rate of investment in the project, arguments which Smith had lost. He had probably not endeared himself to the others by the uncompromising vigour of his views and his usual obstinacy — his fellow directors called him "the most obstinate man between the four seas." It seems more likely that the partners, seeing the works established and at last running profitably, sought to increase their profits further by replacing Smith by a manager employed at a much smaller salary, thus saving the managing director's share of the profits.

Many of those in Coalville and Leicester who knew the inside story thought Smith a fool. Three years before it had been his volatile temperament that had caused his downfall; this time it was mainly his carelessness over his contract, allied to his natural stubborness, that was to cost him and his family dear. For a man who often stated that the security of his wife and family was his chiefest care, Smith was curiously insensitve to the effect of his actions upon them. At several crucial points in his life he proved unable to control his temper or temper his pride. He also seemed unwilling to seek an accommodation in difficult situations and then confrontations followed. He could shrug off the results of his behaviour — loss of employment, income and friends — but they bore hardly upon his wife and children. "The Lord will provide" may have been his comfortable watchword through life, but his family were to suffer long periods of poverty and hardship when the Lord was not in a giving mood.

So once again he lost horse, carriage and coachman, and his first-class season ticket too. With no money coming in and considerable fixed expenses, including a high rent, the Smiths were forced to dismiss their servants. Determined to retain his house as long as possible, Smith sold his diamond rings and then his furniture, piece by piece. He reckoned later that some £300 worth of furniture was either auctioned or sold. At last he reached the stage when he could now longer pay his rent and the bailiffs were constant visitors. He was finally forced to leave the comforts of Dial House. No one, it seems, was willing to rent him a decent property, so after some difficulty he found an empty and dilapidated house in what he euphemistically refers to as "Lovingscote Road" in his *Open Letter*. The walls of his new home were damp, and water and snow trickled in through holes in the roof. To this depressing new home he brought his family and what was left of their possessions.

So deeply unpopular had Smith become, that even here he was pursued by his former partners. Eager to run this turbulent character out of Coalville, indeed out of England altogether, they proposed that if he would leave the country they would keep his wife and children. Smith indignantly refused, telling them: "I had right and truth on my side, and I should not leave the country if it were full of devils and crocodiles before my work and plans for the poor children were brought a more satisfactory issue."

Undeterred by these hammer-blows of fate, he determined to carry on with his crusade on behalf of the canal boat children even though he was again unemployed and virtually penniless. Smith did not realise it at the time but this was to be the beginning of a period of direst poverty for him and his family. Unable to find a suitable post in the area, he was reduced to running up bills for necessities where he could still obtain credit. As for his travelling expenses, he now had to rely on occasional gifts of money from friends and supporters. Later he reflected, "God only knows how we lived, or starved, from 1875 to 1879, and during 1884". He paints a sorry picture of their domestic life:

> Ten cwt. of coal had to last three months which was certainly none too much in the winter. Occasionally I had only one shirt which my wife repaired at times while I lay in bed without one. My little girls used to be dressed in frocks made out of my old tattered and worn waterproof and other coats, and our meat for many long months consisted of a sheep's head which my wife bought every Saturday night, and which was cut into four quarters — one quarter was boiled on each of the first four days, and the bones left made up the fifth day's dinner. Boiled milk or porridge served for the sixth and seventh day's dinners. Our Christmas dinner has more than once been of bread and skim milk.

On this miserable diet the family staggered through the winter, always under the shadow of bankruptcy. This became a reality the following year when, following pressure from his creditors, Smith was made bankrupt. Thanks to the generosity of several friends who settled his debts, Smith was able to obtain his discharge two years later.

It is quite obvious that during these difficult years it was Mary Smith who kept the family together. Smith made a little money from occasional commissions and from looking after and letting the public hall in the town, but it was Mary who managed their meagre resources. She scrimped and saved to provide hot meals for them all, she made the clothes for the growing children, and it was she who endured the cold, damp, unattractive house and tried to provide a semblance of home comfort during Smith's lengthy visits to London. Smith rarely refers to her activities or qualities except when he writes of the warmth and cheer he encounters on returning home. It is true that very occasionally he refers to her admiration and love for him and her faith in his work for the children, but one cannot help feeling that he rather takes all this for granted, as befits an Old Testament figure. This is the domestic and financial background we should keep in mind when we are dealing with Smith's activities — travelling, lobbying, writing, visiting — during the years of his campaign on behalf of the canal boat children.

Chapter 10: The Canal Campaign: Opening Salvos

"Life on a barge is one of the idyllic pictures of English experience. It is compassed about with great calm."

The Times 4 June, 1877.

The canal people were a race apart, rather like the gypsies. Smith often referred to them as "floating gypsies". They were a closed community, suspicious of outsiders, constantly on the move and living largely isolated from the mainstream of industrial life. Since they led this unusual nomadic existence, they did not fall within the jurisdiction of any local authority. Factory Acts did not affect them, and those Acts prohibiting Sunday work or the employment of women and young children did not apply to the canals. Perhaps because they were not directly under the eye of the public, their condition, unlike their reputation, went unnoticed or ignored by MPs, reformers, novelists, and canal company directors. Smith was the first man to show concern about the life led by the women and children working the boats and to draw their plight to the attention of the country.

Smith had personal experience of conditions on the canals: "I have helped to load hundreds of them with bricks in the depths of winter and it was while melting my frozen fingers at the cabin fires that my eyes were opened to the sad condition of the poor canal children." He continued to be a close observer of life on the canals after he left Clayhills. To understand those aspects of the canal children's existence which excited his sympathy and aroused his anger, let us examine the conditions under which the boatmen and their families lived and worked, and indicate the scale of the problem.

No one knows very much about the origin of the boatmen and women in the Canal Age — roughly the eighty years before 1840. Some were probably former 'navigators' or 'navvies', the men who actually dug and constructed the canals and then became boatmen when that work dried up. Others, no doubt, were former 'river-men' who thought that life aboard a canal boat

Narrow boats on the Regent Canal in 1823

offered a softer option. It is probable that a large number were simply recruited from those living and working in the farms, villages and small towns along the route of the canal. Such men as carters and small tenant farmers with their experience of horses and wagons would be likely candidates.

What is certain is that a considerable minority were of gypsy origin and there is some evidence to support this. It is not too fanciful to see a strong resemblance between a boat-cabin and the gypsy van introduced into Europe in the latter half of the eighteenth century. The lay-out of the boat-cabin resembles the gypsies' solution to the problems of living in a confined space. This might also account for the traditional paintings of roses and castles that decorate the outside of the cabin and other parts of the hull. These point to a possible origin in Eastern Europe and the Balkans. The Romany connection is further suggested by the highly-polished brass and metal, the gleaming brass rails, door-knobs and stove chimneybands visible in the better-kept boats. But here romance comes to an end.

During the Canal Age the family boat was very rare. Most narrow boats during this period were crewed by men whose families lived ashore. When the canal companies were forced to cut their cargo rates because of increasing competition from the railways, the wages of the boatmen fell considerably. Their solution was to give up paying rent for a cottage and bring their families on board; this had the added advantage of providing a ready-made crew. It was only on the narrow canals or 'cuts' that these family boats were found. Their trips lasted, as a rule, for about ten days. The boats were constantly on the move, Sundays included, except for the periods spent loading and unloading. The only time the boats were idle was when the canals were frozen up, and even then the families remained on board. Working conditions for the barges on the broad canals and rivers were quite different. In general they were only engaged on short journeys and thus the crews were able to live ashore.

By the middle of the nineteenth century the canal system in England was virtually complete and the Midlands, with its network of narrow canals, was the heart of that system. The canal barges which Smith saw at Tunstall and elsewhere were the traditional 'narrow boats', by far the most numerous type of canal craft on the inland waterways. The majority of boatmen did not own their boats but worked for various canal companies. The boats were cheap to build and economical in terms of the quantity of water required — a vital factor. 'Narrow boat' was the usual term for them throughout the Midlands but they were often called 'monkey boats' in the London area.

They were indeed narrow, with a beam of slightly less than 7ft. and a length of about 70 ft. When they entered a narrow lock there was just enough space to slip a hand between the hull of the boat and the side of the lock. They were capable of carrying up to thirty tons of cargo and were normally horse-drawn, although mules and donkeys were sometimes used. The horse had a special harness ending in a wooden stretcher with a hook that took the eye of the tow-rope. This line ran to a towing-mast rising about 4 ft above the boat's side. Steam-driven narrow boats did not appear on the canals until 1880.

Most of the readers of this book will have seen converted narrow boats used as floating homes or holiday craft and watched them passing through locks. Older readers may remember seeing working boats for a time after the Second World War. It is important to realise when looking at a converted narrow boat today that in most cases the cabin area at the stern behind the engine used to be the living quarters of the boatman and his family, with adults and children crowded into one tiny space, hugger-mugger. It was here that the boatman and his family lived their enclosed, isolated life. In this small space they cooked, ate, slept, made love and gave birth.

There are narrow boats preserved in canal and boat museums today complete with their traditional cabins. These changed little over the years. Let us imagine entering the cabin through the highly-decorated doors at the stern. The interior is about eight and a half feet long, six and a half feet wide and five feet high. Every inch of space is utilised. A small coal range is situated on the left; facing it on the right is a bunk or locker which serves as a seat by day and a bed by night and was called a 'side-bed' by the boatmen. Next to the stove is a crockery cupboard cum larder, the lid of which is hinged at the base and folds down to make a small table for meals. Beyond the table and the side-bed, the 'cross-bed' lies athwart the boat, forming the lid of a deep cupboard where the bedding is stowed. Small shelves, cupboards and lockers make use of the remaining space. It was in these "hot, damp, close, buggy, filthy and stinking holes" that the boatman and his family lived cribb'd, cabin'd and confin'd.

The stench in these cabins must have been quite overpowering, especially when they were infested with bugs. Sometimes the state of a cabin became unendurable, even to the hardened occupants, and the family was forced to fumigate it. They called this process 'bug-driving' or 'smoking them out'. First, they took out all the bedding and cooking utensils and piled them on the tow-path. Next, they stopped all the cracks and openings with soft clay, stopped up the chimney with a large turf and threw a tarpaulin over the cabin. Then several pounds of brimstone were burned inside, while the family waited on the tow-path or on the wharf until the 'bugging' process was complete. This was quite a common sight along the canals.

Smith had no illusions about the people whose children he intended to

Plan of a narrow boat cabin

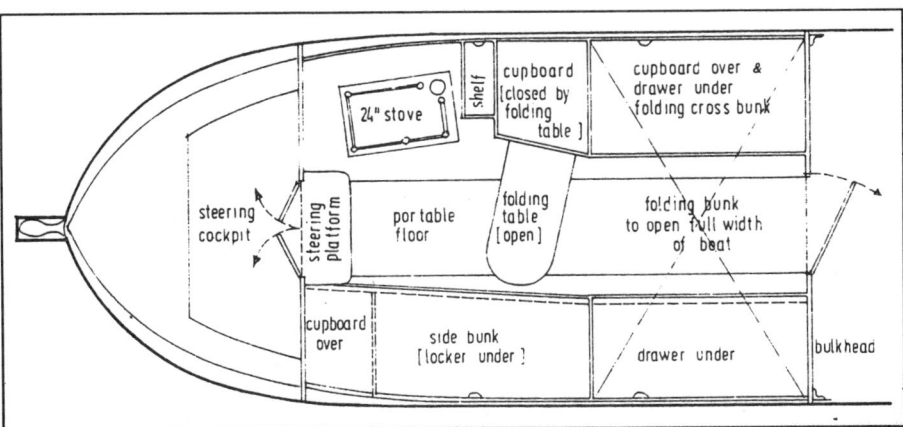

Cabin interior from the bed

help. He considered the boatmen to be more ignorant, more drunken and more abusive than the men working in the brick-yards. Perhaps their freedom of movement and their mode of life in a close-knit community gave them a kind of aggressive independence which the brick-yard employees could neither equal nor afford. The boatmen were easily identified as they lounged about the canal-side by their garb of thick corduroy trousers secured by a broad leather belt, plush waistcoat, great hob-nailed boots (ideal for giving opponents a good kicking) and their much-favoured fur hats.

Smith condemned them as idle, ignorant, vicious brutes whose ruling passion was drink. When inflamed by the demon drink, they were much given to fighting among themselves and brutalising their families. Heavy drinking, of course, was common to much of the labouring population. As for the boatmen, the nature of their work, their appalling living conditions and the lack of other diversions, drew them inevitably towards the public house. This was reflected in the number of low public houses found along the canals which did, literally, roaring business on Sundays. A typical one was described as:

> the grimiest of low-ceilinged tap-rooms, a truly savage and barbaric 'tap' wherein is dispatched the thinnest and flattest beer I have ever yet come across. This is the bargee's usual tipple, for rum is only a special drink for great occasions. Greasy wooden 'settles' and battered wooden tables

furnish the apartment and there come the jolly boatmen to make merry. The walls have two distinct and clearly defined rows of black lines indicating the presence of greasy backs and heads.

In these sordid surroundings the jolly boaters amused themselves by singing dirty songs when sober and sentimental ballads when drunk, interspersed with a little step dancing (at which they were surprisingly adept) to the accompaniment of a fiddle or concertina.

The boatmen showed as little concern for their horses as they did for their children, despite the important part animals played in their work. Horses and donkeys were regarded by most of them in the same light as children and treated as cruelly and casually. The animals spent their nights either in canal-side stables, if they were lucky, or simply tethered on the bank. The horses were usually broken-down hunters, post-horses or cab-horses approaching the end of their working life. Smith once met a ragged seven-year old girl leading a large horse along the towing-path. In her right hand was a loose bridle, which hung sufficiently low to enable the child, dripping wet with rain and sleet, to guide the horse. With a "Gee up, you old beast!" and a stroke across the horse's fore-legs with a heavy whip, she urged him along. Every few yards the man at the tiller would curse the child and shout, "Now then, give it to him. Shove him along or I'll come and pitch you both in the cut."

Smith considered that the women reflected the callousness and squalor which were their everyday lot, and as a result were as coarse, dirty and foul-mouthed as their husbands. They were not a very attractive sight in their short blue cotton frocks and laced-up heavy boots, with a bonnet like a quilted cowl which hung in flaps on their shoulders. Smith recalled that he had often seen the boat-women strip and fight like men, biting and kicking and pulling each other's hair by by the roots. He had also observed them half-naked, leaning over the side of the boat as it went along and washing themselves in the canal. This is hardly surprising since they washed their clothes in water from the canal, cooked with it and often drank it.

The morality of the boatmen and their wives has been not unfairly compared with that of their contemporaries living in the worst slums in Liverpool and Manchester. Their children could hardly avoid being contaminated by the behaviour of their parents and by the conditions under which they slept. At night, boys and girls of varying ages slept with their parents in what Smith called "these hell-holes". There might be as many as two adults and up to five or six children crowded together. When Smith enquired how they managed it, one boatman replied succinctly, "Like pigs, all of a heap". Another said, "One child at the head of the father and mother and another at their feet, and the rest on the sideseat and on the floor". In such a nasty and unsavoury nest overcrowding at night offered opportunities for beastliness. Smith referred in blunt terms that shocked many of his Victorian readers to cases where "girls of seventeen give birth to children, the fathers of which are members of their own family."

The boatmen and their wives displayed an unusual lack of feeling towards their children and showed no interest in easing their hardships. For example, it was common practice among the boaters to lend children to another boat or even give them away altogether. A reporter from the *Warrington Guardian* stumbled across an example of this on a visit to Runcorn:

> I walked on to the canal bank at Runcorn and jumped onto the first boat alongside the wharf. Its cabin accommodation was very bad indeed. There was a woman on board and I asked her how many children she had. She replied that she had one of her own and one given to her. 'Given to you?' I said, 'What do you mean?' 'Well, this 'ere lad', said the woman of a lad about twelve years of age, 'he was gin to me'.

The fate of many of those children who were loaned, given away or sent to work at a tender age for another boatman hardly bears thinking about.

When the children were about seven or eight years old they were put to steering the boat, driving the horse and later, when they were strong enough, opening and closing the locks. As they grew up, the boys usually followed in their fathers' footsteps. By the time they became boatmen they were quite experienced in loading and unloading cargo, working with animals, swearing, drinking and thieving. The girls, given the nature of this traditional community, tended to marry other boatmen. Soon there would be two or three little ones in the cabin and the vicious circle began again, with the children growing up as illiterate and ignorant as previous generations.

Such was the picture of canal life that Smith painted in his speeches, letters and articles. He was certainly justified in drawing the public's attention to the disgusting conditions in the cabins, the widespread drunkenness and the ignorance of the children. But, as in the case of the brick-yard workforce, several of Smith's statements and allegations about the canal folk must be treated with considerable reserve. Sincere though he was, Smith was intent on making as strong a case as possible and one that would excite public sympathy. Yet his wholesale condemnation of the boatmen and their wives hardly stands up to examination. It is true that canal boatmen had a fearsome reputation, but they were not all drunken, vicious, illiterate brutes with wives who were not much better. As a class they had no monopoly of sin and their womenfolk were in many cases more sinned against than sinning. A woman in Paddington once remarked to Smith: "The boatman who first put a woman into a boat deserved hanging". Furthermore, Smith's accusations were made in his highly-coloured, hyperbolic style which, though accepted by many at their face value, were considered grossly over-stated by those with some knowledge of the canals and their floating population. As Smith later admitted, there were many kind-hearted and respectable couples working on the canals and living in clean and well-kept cabins. Such families, however, rarely make good copy and bad reputations once established prove difficult to dispel.

Cabin interior from the door

Because of their wandering occupation, it is hard to obtain accurate figures of the number of boat people working on the canals. Smith originally claimed that there were some 80,000 to 100,000 people but this was a wild exaggeration and he was to revise it downwards more than once. If we interpret the figures thrown up by the Census returns of 1871 and 1891, it seems much more likely that the total of those living on canal boats (excluding children under five) was about 30,000. Thus the number of children was probably between 6,000 and 7,000. To put matters in perspective, this figure was roughly a quarter to a third of the number of children Smith found working in the brick-fields a few years earlier. But this forgotten class of children, condemned to a wretched existence in an environment of ignorance, squalor and ill-usage, had at last found a doughty champion.

Smith began his campaign in October 1873 by writing letters to the national and provincial press seeking their support for his work. At this stage he avoided dealing with immorality and drunkenness and concentrated instead on two major issues: first, the shocking living conditions in the boat-cabins, where a space estimated at just over 200 cubic feet had to provide a home for four to seven persons; and secondly, the need to educate the children. It was a sympathetic cause; Smith's reputation was now such that his letters aroused considerable interest and support. He was not able to follow this up at once because his recent appointment as managing director of the Northend Brick and Tile Company occupied most of his time. So he did nothing publicly for several months, apart from collecting evidence about conditions on the canals as and when he could.

He broke his unnatural silence on the subject at Moira in Leicestershire on 27 April, 1874, when he addressed a public meeting held in a tent to celebrate a local Sunday School anniversary. Moira was an important canal basin on the Ashby-de-la-Zouch canal some eight miles west of Coalville. He amused his audience by relating how, a few days before, he had met the director of a local colliery. When Smith told him he would shortly be visiting Moira and asked him if he could give him any information about the boat children, the man rounded angrily on him and said, "If you come to Moira, I will see that you have a ducking, for it is people like you going about the country that causes men to be dissatisfied with their condition".

Smith then became serious and voiced his concern about the shocking conditions for children in the boat cabins, urged a Parliamentary enquiry, and suggested the Factory and Workshop Act of 1871 might be brought to bear upon the problem. Smith gave several telling examples of what he had found, including a visit to one boat cabin in which lived a man, his wife and six children, one of the girls being 16, another 14, with a lad of 10 and little ones. "A man, his wife and six children, and only one room for everything!" People with families knew what that meant. His Moira speech was widely reported and he was soon being referred to as the 'Boatmen's Friend'. Extensive press coverage followed during the summer with more emphasis being being placed upon the need for education. So rapid was the response to Smith's pleas that in December the *Leicester Daily Post* was able to hint that "a measure for the protection of these children is to form one of the subjects which the Government will ask Parliament to deal with next session".

The momentum was increasing and early in the New Year Smith was invited by John Morley to contribute a lengthy article to the February issue of his influential *Fortnightly Review*. In this Smith described the canal population as "perhaps the most debased of our serf class" and described the noisome conditions under which they lived. He inveighed against the habits of the boatmen and their wives (with examples!) and the way they neglected to send their children either to school or Sunday School.

It should not be assumed from Smith's strictures that no efforts had been made to provide basic education for the boat-children and that no organisation had been set up to bring religion to the waterways. The problem with most schools of this period was their reluctance, or outright refusal, to admit boat-children because of their appearance and reputation. But there were, in fact, a few schools along the canals established specially for the boatmen's children. These were built either by private individuals or by public subscription, but only a tiny proportion of the boat-children attended, and this small number only came irregularly.

There was also a variety of well-intentioned efforts to cater for the spiritual needs of the boatmen and their families. It was no easy task dealing with such a transient congregation. One or two canal companies supported boats fitted out as floating chapels. In Chester, for example, the Shropshire Union Canal Company and the Duke of Westminster paid for a boat with a spire, designed to collect the boatmen and their families together for worship, and to serve as a school for the children. The Weaver Navigation Company went further and built three churches in the 1840's at Weston Point (where their river joined the Mersey), at Northwich and at Winsford, and paid for parsons, singers, cleaners and hymn books. At each place they also established schools for the children of those who worked on the navigation, and paid the teachers.

One of the earliest and most successful attempts to bring religion to the canals was the establishment of the Boatmen's Mission in 1846. This had its headquarters at Paddington and developed branches at such important canal basins as Birmingham, Worcester, Droitwich and Tipton. The Mission provided a chapel for boatmen and their wives with Sunday and week-day services, and also free Day and Sunday Schools for the children. Here again the missionaries found it difficult, despite visiting boats regularly, to attract the children to either. Smith made a trenchant comment upon their activities:

"What is the good of sending city missionaries among the boaters to read a chapter or two out of the Bible, on top of the cabin, to one or two old folk, while there are hundreds of boat-children around them not taught to read and write and fear God?"

Chapter 11: Winning Ways and Winter Walks

> "Last spring I questioned some boat-children as to whether they had ever heard of Jesus Christ. "No', said one, 'He has never been along this cut — what sort of a chap is He?'"
>
> George Smith: *Our Canal Population*

By early 1875, having given up both his Sunday School work and his political activity, Smith had plenty of time to prepare the book he hoped would clinch his canal campaign with its convincing and unassailable deployment of facts and figures. *Our Canal Population: A Cry from the Boat Cabins* came out later in the year. Very similar to his previous work, *The Cry of the Children from the Brickyards of England,* it was not a book as generally understood but rather a compilation. It consisted of a brief introduction outlining his main concerns, followed by a thinly-veiled attack on the Church of England for its indifference and indolence. After this came various letters, articles and reports of his speeches cobbled together from the national and provincial press with much repetition and wordy irrelevance.

There were one or two differences compared with *The Cry*. Here he was not concerned with the exploitation of children by unscrupulous owners and manufacturers, with their long, exhausting hours of manual work, and the casual violence meted out to them in the workplace. Instead he concentrated on their exposure to immorality and disease as a result of their appalling living conditions. Actually, there is no evidence to support his claim that infectious and contagious diseases were rife in the cabins and that the boats were responsible for transmitting disease from town to town. He also considered the children to be stunted and unhealthy. This was quite at variance with medical opinion. Boatmen, their wives and children, despite the state of the cabins, tended to be remarkably healthy, perhaps because of their isolation and their outdoor life on the waterways.

Smith was not the man to be unduly disturbed by lack of evidence to support his assertions. He knew he had a good case that had already attracted much attention and, as in the case of his first book, he circulated copies of

Our Canal Population as widely as possible — and at his own expense.

Earlier in the year, in February, Smith had been delighted and perhaps a little surprised to be invited to read a paper on "Church work among the Boatmen" at the Church Congress at Stoke-on-Trent in October. Smith arrived in the town a few days before the conference only to be told by the organisers that objections had been raised to his taking part in the Church Congress and that someone else had been invited to read a paper on the subject. Smith was astonished and hurt. It seems that, following his arrival in Stoke, the Committee had made some enquiries about his religious sentiments and learned to their horror they had unknowingly invited a hyperactive Nonconformist to share their platform. Smith's paper was immediately expunged from the conference programme.

There was an outcry in the local press at his shabby treatment and, as had happened before, this led to his paper being widely published by sympathetic journals. In fact, his paper turned out to be a sermon more than anything else, and more of a diatribe than a sermon. It was construed as an attack upon the failure of the Church of England to do anything for the canal people and in it we see the Primitive Methodist at work. Smith laid about him with a will, castigating the Church for apathy and lack of evangelical fervour:

> Sermons as dry and lifeless as stones will not reach their hearts. To do this, the minister must have his heart fired by the Holy Spirit as by electricity from the source of all light and heat.... Plain language out of the plain old Book, spoken by men who know how to touch the heart is what the boatmen desire... It is the duty of the Church to see that men and women living in boats as men and wives in an unmarried state are married; that drunkards become sober, that habits of industry, cleanliness, honesty and frugality are encouraged, and that children are baptised. Has it done this? We say, No, not as it might have been done. The church has been like a child, content to play with toys while it ought to have been doing the hard, if perhaps unpleasant, work of seeking for the stray sheep on our waterways and barges. Instead of standing by while the boatmen are sinking, it should have sent out the life-boat. Of course, I am only speaking of the Church and its work among boatmen and their families. What it has done in other parts of the vineyard I must leave for others to show.

It was just as well that Smith did not address the Congress in person because there were all the ingredients in his inflammatory address for a genteel clerical riot. He might well have either emptied the hall or been shouted down by an angry crowd of silver-haired parsons. Even if Smith's imagery was somewhat confusing, the message was clear and unequivocal: "The Church must be up and doing, and do her part, and that not a little." These sentiments and the language in which they were couched were not likely to endear Smith to the Church of England. He was never invited to address their Congress again.

Smith was in touch with his friend Robert Baker and Baker's colleague, Captain May, over his efforts to bring the plight of the boat-children before the public. They mentioned these in their annual report for 1875, at the same time condemning the conditions under which the children were brought up as a national disgrace. Meanwhile, Smith had tried to induce the Factory and Workshops Act Commission to look into the problem, despite the fact that boat cabins were neither factories nor workshops. He managed to persuade Sir James Ferguson, the chairman, to let him present his case and he was invited to a meeting of the Commission in Leicester on 21 June. Smith now had the opportunity to put forward the simple proposals he had been developing In his letters and articles for the last eighteen months and which he hoped might one day form the basis of a Parliamentary Bill. He did so in his usual cogent and persuasive manner. He also referred to the detailed statement which he had already sent to the members about the state of the canal population and his suggestions for its improvement.

His remedies included the following: no boys under thirteen and girls under eighteen to sleep or work on boats; a maximum space of seventy-five cubic feet for each adult above eighteen, and fifty cubic feet for each youth between thirteen and eighteen; the name of the boat-owner, together with the name of the captain, to be painted on each boat, and boats to be properly registered as to the amount of tonnage carried and the number of persons allowed to live and sleep on board; inspectors to be appointed with adequate powers, and the age of each child to be proved by certificates duly signed by the parish authorities. The Commission was impressed by Smith's performance. Although in its next report it excluded the canal population from consideration in terms of factory legislation, at least it recommended the introduction of regulations prohibiting "the residence in canal boats of female young persons (i.e. girls up to the age of 18) and of children above the age of three years." This was a significant step forward.

Although Smith was strictly *persona non grata* with the Church of England, the Social Science Association were only too happy to offer him a platform. Early in 1876 he was invited to address their autumn Congress at

Liverpool. The second part of his paper dealt with the inspection of canal boats. It may be thought that Smith was putting the cart before the horse in discussing methods of inspection and enforcement before the legislative process had got under way, but he realised from his previous experience that these matters were the core of any successful Act. His speech went over much familiar ground first and it was only in the last few minutes that he actually dealt with the question of inspecting canal boats. It would, he claimed, be both easy and cheap. It merely required two inspectors, one stationed at Birmingham to deal with the Midlands and all the canals south and east, the other stationed at Manchester responsible for all the canals north and west of Birmingham. They would not only look after the children but would inspect the boats and canals and report where life and property were in danger. He added as an afterthought, and a provocative afterthought it proved, that Sunday travelling —except in special cases— should be done away with, thus giving the boat people a rest and the chance to attend church or chapel.

Smith now considered the various options open to him to achieve his end. In view of the reluctance of the Local Government Board to become involved in helping the canal boat children, he still hankered after a Royal Commission charged with the sole aim of enquiring into the condition of the canal population. Despite the success of previous commissions in highlighting abuses in various industries, he soon found there was little parliamentary appetite for yet another one. Besides, a Commission would cost over £2,000!

He reckoned there were one or two Acts which might serve his purpose and for a time he pursued the possibilities offered by Lord Sandon's Education Act (1876). This measure, aimed directly at improving school attendance, placed the onus of ensuring a child received an efficient elementary education firmly upon the parent. Smith's suggestions along these lines, however, were not favourably received. As a last resort he tried to get a suitable clause inserted in the Merchant Shipping Bill recently brought in by the Government, but again he was unsuccessful. The Home Secretary (Richard Cross) finally informed him he could do nothing about the matter for the time being and that any legislation would have to wait until the next session. Smith correctly interpreted this as a discreet shelving of his proposals.

Yet, nothing daunted, Smith kept up the pressure and on 15th January, 1877, one of his supporters, asked the Home Secretary in the House if the

Government intended to bring in legislation soon to give effect to the recommendation of the Factory Commissioners that "the residence in canal boats of female young persons, and children above the age of three years should be forbidden". This produced an anodyne response from Cross, at once praising Smith's efforts but refusing to adopt all the Report's suggestions. He did concede, however, that if persons slept on board, then the boats should be registered in much the same way as lodging houses.

But the point had been made, and a little later Cross invited Smith to the Home Office to discuss the provisions of a draft Bill. Smith was happy at the way in which the problems were now being addressed and even more delighted when Cross told him that the Bill would be brought in shortly by Mr. Sclater-Booth, the President of the Local Government Board, mainly because there was not enough time for witnesses to be called and examined to enable the Select Committee to present its report before the Parliamentary recess. The Bill did not meet all Smith's requirements but he was anxious to see it on the Statute Book, feeling that "a piece of the loaf is better than none".

The Canal Boats Bill was brought in on 24 May and read a first time. But in June, on the motion of the House going into Committee on the Bill, Mr. Rylands, the MP for Burnley, moved that it should be referred to a Select Committee. Smith saw in this the hand of the Canal Association who, like the brick-yard owners before them, were apprehensive about the effects of legislation. The opponents of the Bill failed to halt its progress, despite the efforts of Staveley Hill MP, QC, who had been instructed by the Canal Association to oppose the Bill at every stage. He told Smith to his face that "he would move heaven and earth to throw the Bill out." Nevertheless, the Bill was passed by the Select Committee on 10th July providing for "the Registration and Regulation of Canal Boats used as Dwellings". Staveley Hill was not the man to give up easily. A fortnight later he proposed that the Bill should be re-committed to the Select Committee, and he found an ally in that formidable figure and noted obstructionist, Parnell, who attempted to have the Bill talked out.

Smith heard about this tactic, left home by an early train and hurried to the Commons. He was in time to enjoy a memorable twenty-six hours' sitting at the end of which Sclater-Booth successfully moved the third reading. Opposition to the Bill collapsed and on 14th August it received the Royal assent. That night Smith summed up his feelings in his diary:

> Thank God! thank God! Oh, how thankful I feel! During the last four years' work among the canal boatmen, and in getting the Act, scandal, lies, persecution, temptation, aching head, sleepless nights, insults, snubs, hunger, fatigue and poverty have been my lot and that of my wife and family.... Many times my little darlings could not go to school for want of shoes; the whole of us have had scarcely more linen than we carried on our backs, and that almost in rags; red herrings for Sunday's dinner more than once; tea, or rather warm water without sugar for breakfast, which had to be drunk out of cups, mugs, or basins, odds and ends of old crockery, no two pieces alike. Damp walls, bad roof, broken chairs and tables have been our lot. And thus have we gone along without a penny in our pockets, but trusting in Providence.

On 1st January, 1878, the Canal Boats Act came into operation. In future all boats were to be registered and the registration authorities were empowered to fix the number, age and sex of all persons who might be allowed to live in a boat. Local sanitary authorities were to inspect the boats for infectious diseases. As for elementary education, a school attendance committee in the registration areas would assume responsibility for the boat children. The Act also empowered the canal companies to set up schools for children of their employees while the registration authorities were given complete powers to initiate inspection in the enforcement of the Act's provisions, exercised through the usual sanitary authorities.

One unspoken purpose of the Act was to encourage local authorities to put improvements in hand without too much pressure from central government or the imposition of stringent regulations. Thus the Act was a permissive measure only (shades of Smith's Brick-yard Act) and all efforts at enforcement were left to the sanitary authorities. During the months after the passing of the Act Smith looked in vain for efforts being made to stamp out the abuses it was designed to eliminate. Many local authorities did very little beyond registering the boats to be used as dwellings, largely ignoring the regulations introduced by the Local Government Board later in the year.

The major failings of the Act Smith had pointed out earlier were now becoming all too clear: its permissive nature, the lack of enforcement, the non-annual registration of boats and the failure of the educational clauses. Angry at the lack of progress, he determined to find out for himself the extent of the problems and who was at fault. He decided to walk the canal between Rugby and London while the canal was frozen up to gather information about the operation of the Act and the condition of the boatmen and their families. Dissatisfied and downhearted at the events — or non-events — of the year, Smith gave way to one of his fits of depression. He confessed to his diary on Christmas Eve:

> At home some part of the day, playing with my fingers, and feeling terribly miserable. It will take me all my time in the midst of heartless cruel opposition, a relentless world, pecuniary difficulties, bad trade, hard times, comfortless home, lean fare, and an empty pocket, to find my way to heaven.

But first he had to make his way to Rugby. After a sombre and cheerless Christmas with his family, he left home on the 23th December 1878 with his "carpet bag in one hand and a great shaggy coat in the other." He travelled by train from Coalville to Rugby via Leicester and there he stumped off across the fields through the snow and slush to start his journey south.

Dedication to Canal Adventures by Moonlight

TO THE

RIGHT HONOURABLE
SIR WILLIAM VERNON HARCOURT, M.P.,

HER MAJESTY'S SECRETARY OF STATE

FOR THE HOME DEPARTMENT;

AND

ALL ENGLISHMEN AND ENGLISHWOMEN,

WHO,

WITH LOVING HEARTS AND WILLING HANDS,

STAND

READY TO HELP FORWARD THE CAUSE OF SUFFERING CHILDREN;

AND ALSO

TO THOSE WHO HAVE HITHERTO SHUT THEIR EYES,

STEELED THEIR HEARTS,

AND TURNED A DEAF EAR TO THE CRIES OF THE LITTLE ONES,

THIS VOLUME IS INSCRIBED BY

THE AUTHOR.

Welton, Daventry,
August 12th, 1881.

Although he had bravely stated that his intention was to walk from Rugby to the canal basin at Paddington, what he did was rather different. He decided to visit the principal canal wharves on the Grand Union Canal. This was a sensible plan because in this way he could examine the maximum number of boats in a short time, especially when the cut was frozen over. He did walk the towpath for some stretches but we find him taking the train from time to time between towns along his route. Because he had so little money for his journey, Smith was forced to stay the night in the cheapest and most dismal lodging houses. He describes these and their owners with a Dickensian vividness. One night he fetched up at a public house not far from the market place at Fenny Stratford.

> I retired to my room, with my feet and stockings wet and as cold as a frozen tramp. My wet boots I left on the floor, but I put my stockings into my grubby bed to dry. The walls of the room had not been cleaned or papered for at least twenty years. At one end of the room some of the old faded paper hung in threads upon a damp wall. My bed lay alongside of another bed.
>
> In going to my room I had to pass through a room with four beds in it and another with two beds in it; altogether the place presented a scene as if navvies had been bedded down by the dozen for threepence a night.

While he was away from home he also ate sparingly and existed on the most meagre of fare — tea, buns, pork pies, ginger beer, bread and cheese — usually taken in dirty canal-side public houses.

Smith found to his irritation that none of the boats he saw as he journeyed southward were registered under the Act. It was not until he reached Brentford on the western outskirts of London that he saw his first registered boat. By this time the thaw had set in and the Paddington basin was a depressing spectacle. Smith was relieved to find a friend of his living nearby who gave him a hearty tea in front of the fire. His various encounters and adventures during his winter journey were to form the first part of his book, *Canal Adventures by Moonlight*, published two and a half years later.

His Winterreise convinced Smith that the situation on the canals had been little affected by the Canal Boats Act. As he was to admit later to the Select Committee on canals, he was very disappointed with the immediate results of his measure: "to a certain extent it has been beneficial but not altogether so." The benefits did not appear to extend very far. The local authorities had done little beyond registering a small number of boats and the overcrowding in the dirty cabins was as bad as ever.

As soon as Smith returned home he began to bombard the London and provincial press with letters, quoting chapter and verse, urging the authorities to make greater efforts to put the Act into operation and to enforce the regulations issued by the Local Government Board during 1878. He also began to put more emphasis on the importance of education in his writings. He reckoned that if he could get the local authorities to register the boats then the children would come under the jurisdiction of the local School Board Officer and would have to attend school.

Smith's labours on behalf of the boat children, especially during his years of poverty, did not go unnoticed or entirely unrewarded. His diary for 4th March 1879 records that he went down to the House of Commons to see his local MP about presenting a petition to the Home Secretary to have the sentence reduced for a man who was serving a life sentence for a poaching affray. It was a typical Smith philanthropic errand. Later that day he ran into John Corbett, the MP for Droitwich, and, while discussing the Canal Boats Act, Corbett told Smith that the Government should have given him the job of carrying out the Act. As it had chosen not to, Smith ought to have something substantial for all the work he had done, such as "two hundred acres of good land in Derbyshire, or some other good county." Smith thought he was joking and replied, "Oh, yes, you mean, I suppose, two hundred acres of land in Zululand or Cyprus." But Corbett meant what he said and he suggested Smith saw Forster, now a

The Canal Boatmen's Magazine

THE

CANAL BOATMEN'S

MAGAZINE,

FOR THE YEAR 1882.

NEW SERIES—VOL. III.

"In meekness instructing those that oppose themselves; if God peradventure will give them repentance to the acknowledging of the truth."—2 Tim. ii. 25.

London:

PUBLISHED BY THE PADDINGTON SOCIETY FOR PROMOTING CHRISTIAN KNOWLEDGE AMONG CANAL BOATMEN AND OTHERS;

And Sold by J. Nisbet, 21, Berners Street; F. Baisler, 124, Oxford Street; or by Mr. Pitts, *Secretary*, 43, Paddington Street.

distinguished elder statesman. To Smith's gratification Forster endorsed Corbett's remarks and organised a meeting for the purpose of making "provision for Mr. Smith's needs sufficient for him to be able to devote his life to philanthropic work without the pressure of anxiety for daily bread".

It took place in March in London at the headquarters of the Social Science Association at 1, Adam Street, Adelphi, under the presidency of Lord Aberdare, the former Home Secretary. Warm tributes were paid to Smith's work, and speaker after speaker stressed that he had virtually beggared himself in his efforts for the children. The meeting agreed to establish a large committee drawn from those eminent peers, MPs, reformers and journalists who had been sympathetic to Smith's efforts since his first campaign. The aim was to raise the sum of five thousand pounds, which would provide a modest competence for Smith and his family for many years.

One of the first contributions was a grant of £50 made from the Royal Bounty at the request of Disraeli in recognition of Smith's work. This gift gave Smith particular pleasure for he naturally assumed that Queen Victoria was at work behind the scenes on his behalf. After this promising start, the fund was to have an unhappy history. Despite the editors of several influential newspapers pushing the claims of a man who had done the state some service, the response was muted. After two years, only one thousand pounds had been subscribed. Some inconclusive squabbling took place among the members of the committee behind the scenes about how best to revive the appeal, but in the end they decided to wind the scheme up. All Smith received was some seven hundred pounds, and that two years later, the rest being swallowed up in 'administrative expenses'.

Chapter 12: An Inland Voyage

> Why do sinners' ways prosper? and why must
> Disappointment all endeavour end?
>   Gerard Manley Hopkins: *Thou Art Indeed Just, Lord.*

During the summer of 1879 Smith continued to make frequent fact-finding visits to the canal basins and wharves in London, because the authorities there had made little or no effort to put the Act into operation. While in London he stayed in lodgings in Montague Street or in Museum Street near the British Museum. He spent an increasing amount of time in the Reading Room there, gathering information, writing hundreds of letters and working up material for his various books. Although this superb structure only opened in 1857, it had already proved something of a refuge for impoverished writers and researchers and the occasional political exile. This free, warm, quiet haven attracted some bizarre characters, often curiously clad, so Smith, with his long hair and unkempt appearance, was not unduly conspicuous. He used the Reading Room unashamedly as his London office and he became well-known to the regulars. He usually sat in the same seat in Row I and, when acquaintances teased him about this, he would reply, "Yes, you will generally find me here, first of the egotists." Smith was all too aware of his failings, though perhaps this one might be forgiven in a man so single-minded in his devotion to children's causes.

His visits to London became more frequent and were normally made when Parliament was sitting. He attended the House regularly, chasing up his Bills and lobbying sympathetic MPs. He became a familiar sight in the precincts of Parliament, especially to those MPs from the Midland constituencies. Parliament sat for fewer months then than it does today and during those long stretches of the year when our legislators were following traditional pursuits on their country estates, journeying abroad, enjoying the London season and spending more time with their families, Smith travelled extensively around canal centres in the Midlands. His shabby figure became well-known to boatmen working between Birmingham and Chesterfield, and to others as well. On one occasion at Derby he met an old friend who took him on one side and said, "George Smith of Coalville, as one who wishes you and the cause of the children you are helping forward God's speed, you look as if you want a new hat. If you won't be offended, allow me to make a present of one to you." Smith accepted it gracefully and handed his old hat to a nearby boatman. Then his friend stood him "a good feed off a first-rate joint in the Midland refreshment room" before Smith caught the train home.

This was not an isolated instance of his down-at-heel appearance and shoulder-length white hair attracting attention. A Welsh member chatting with some friends in the lobby of the House once asked him, with a straight face, if he was a Druid. not realising his leg was being pulled, Smith strenuously denied it, but was so unnerved that "'with Druid ringing in my ears, I bolted for my lodgings". Again, his diary entry for the following year (17th April, 1881) reveals how one day he went to the station and a porter accosted him with: "I think, sir, you wants a different set-out, both in clothes and carpet bags, for a gentleman in your position. With the influence you has in the county, you ought to come out as a first-class gentleman as regards dress." Smith thanked him and crossing over to the opposite platform met a solicitor he knew. The solicitor gave him a £5 note which he had unexpectedly received in settlement of an abandoned debt. This illustrates one of Smith's fervent beliefs that "The Lord will provide." And He did seem to provide when Smith's finances were at a low ebb or at critical points in his career. Help arrived regularly at the eleventh hour. In this case, Smith celebrated by buying himself a new suit.

Smith's next move was to arrange for a question in the House about the progress being made in the registration of boats. Mr. Sclater-Booth, on behalf of the Local Government Board, replied that registration had been effected in two-thirds of the ninety nine districts. Smith found this difficult to believe, and so early in October our intrepid traveller was off again, this time to tour some of the canal districts in Lancashire. In the space of a few days he visited the wharves at Leicester, Derby, Manchester, Blackburn, Burnley, Todmorden and Rochdale. For a change, he was encouraged by what he found. He saw no more than a dozen unregistered boats and he compared the situation in the North-West most favourably with that in London. Even so, Smith found that those clauses of the Act dealing with the education of children and conditions in the cabins were almost totally disregarded. As the *Echo* commented, more in sorrow than in anger, "There is little prospect under the present Act of any change".

The year 1880 was to be one full of incident for Smith and his family, though it started on a sad note. He received news that his old friend and fellow campaigner, Robert Baker, had died in Leamington on 6th February at the age of seventy-six. Baker was buried in York Minster, where a memorial pays tribute to his work. It reads:

> This tablet is erected by the voluntary donations of the certifying surgeons acting under his supervision, to place on record their high appreciation of his private character, of his life-long work in promoting and extending Factory legislation in the interests of the artisan class, and of his wise recognition and persistent advocacy of the medical aspects of the Factory Laws.

Handsome though this is from his old colleagues, one cannot help thinking that Baker's work deserved rather wider recognition.

As Disraeli's Ministry dragged to a close, Smith's friends told him that all would be well with his canal children once there was a change of government. When the Liberals won the election in 1880 and Gladstone, at the age of seventy one, formed his second administration, the same friends were delighted and assured Smith that his cherished Bill would soon be on the statute book. Their optimism was misplaced and short-lived. For the next decade and beyond, Parliamentary affairs were to be dominated by the struggle for Irish Home Rule. Irish Nationalism and Irish obstructionists were to bedevil Parliament, breaking men and governments alike.

The Irish question took up a disproportionate amount of the Government's time and energy. It prevented the passing of urgent social legislation and inevitably restricted the number of Bills from private members. Thus neither Gladstone nor, later, Salisbury were in a position to introduce reforms on the scale of the Liberal and Conservative ministries of the late 'sixties and 'seventies. Smith's plans for what were regarded by many in high places as two minority groups of little economic or political importance were to be affected, though he did not realise as the new decade opened how much delay and disillusionment he was to suffer. Smith did admit later that the Government had its hands full during this period: "Ireland and the Irish at the beginning, Ireland and the Irish in the middle and Ireland and the Irish at the end".

Later in the year Smith made another journey, not quite so dramatically presented as the Winter Journey, but much more interesting. After spending some time in London, he arranged to travel back to Leicester in a narrow boat leaving Paddington Basin on 2nd September. This voyage home took him six days and he celebrated it in the second part of *Canal Adventures by Moonlight* under the heading, *Six Days in a Monkey Boat*. This, I am delighted to record, is a fascinating and well-written account of a journey up the Grand Union canal from Paddington to Leicester, providing us with an accurate picture of life on a busy canal.

His boat, called the *Ouse*, was heavily laden with a heady cargo of rice, leather, paraffin, hemp-seed and oil. On the first evening they reached Rickmansworth just as it was growing dark and, since there was no room in the boat for Smith, he eventually found a bed in a house on the wharf bank. The owner earned his living by looking after the horses tied up in his stable for the night and in selling home-made "rice pudden and ginger beer" — and nothing else! Smith noted:

> The 'rice pudden' is made in a tin about three inches deep and about a foot square, without eggs or cream. 'Skim dick' with plenty of sugar and rice are the component parts of the pudding, which is cut into pieces about three inches square after being baked rather hard. These are sold to the factory girls for breakfast, as they pass the house in the morning, at one penny per square.

For a couple of nights Smith found himself sleeping amidships on large lumpy bags of rice. On the other nights he slept in lodgings similar to the dreary ones he had used on his winter journey. He records a range of canal characters he met on the way and his encounters with them and also with lodging house keepers. One of the characters he came across was an eighty-five year old boatman known as 'Ben the legger' because he had spent more than fifty years legging boats through Braunston tunnel. 'Legging' entails lying on your back on a board about 12 inches wide and 3 feet long, outrigged from the side of the boat and called a 'wing'; and pushing with your feet against the tunnel walls to work the boat along. Ben never allowed his wife to live in the cabin and he deplored the overcrowding in many boats. "For the life of me I canna tell how they packs 'em in. There inna enough room for them to stand up, much more to lie down."

Smith left the *Ouse* and his friends at Leicester, but no sooner was he home than he was busy preparing an address about the inspection of canal boats for the Social Science Congress at Edinburgh on 1st October. He drew particular attention to overcrowding in the cabins, quoting the following examples:

At Leicester I found a boat upon which were man, wife, and six children, some grown up.

On one boat I visited near Rickmansworth, there slept in one cabin, four men, one woman and four children. Neither men, woman, nor children could read a sentence or write a letter.

On two other boats I saw near Watford, there were man, woman, and eight sons and daughters of all ages and sizes; not one of them could tell a letter.

I was at Oakthorpe Colliery in Derbyshire, a few days since, and found overcrowding in the cabins as bad, if not worse, than it was before the passing of the Act. The manager told me that there were living in one cabin 'either nine or eleven of both sexes, and of all shapes and sizes', and poor, dirty, sickly creatures they looked.

In the middle of October Smith decided to leave "his wretched nest" in Coalville for good. It had been the scene of much bitterness and unhappiness in recent years, with Smith and his family being ostracised and humiliated. He had thought about moving for some time and, during his return from London on the *Ouse,* he made up his mind that living in the heart of the canal country would benefit his work for the children and also provide a happier and more attractive environment for his family. He found an old, thatched farm-cottage to rent for twelve pounds per annum in the pleasant village of Welton near Daventry. The village climbs up the side of a steep winding hill to a ridge with extensive views over the Northamptonshire countryside. Smith found it "surrounded by fine large trees, lovely fields, pleasant lanes and warm-hearted friends." It was also noted, he observes, for its fat women. He carried his few sticks of furniture and meagre possessions there in a cart, because he was too embarrassed to have his battered belongings sent by rail. The journey via Lutterworth took him several days. Having unloaded the contents of the cart into South View, 14 Ashby Road, he returned to Coalville to collect his family. A few days later the Smiths waited on a deserted station for the train to bear them away from the town Mary had come to detest. Smith's sister was the only person in Coalville on the platform to say goodbye and wish them well.

There is an amusing postscript to this move. Smith was enormously proud of his territorial title 'of Coalville' and was determined to retain it. No sooner had he and his family settled into their new home than he wrote to the Queen explaining that he still wished to be known as 'George Smith of Coalville' despite his change of address. His new home soon became known

South View, 14 Ashby Road, Welton, Northants. The thatched roof had long been replaced by a corrugated iron one when this photograph was taken.

as 'Coalville House'. Nothing of it remains today; it was demolished to make way for a more desirable property. It was in these pleasant, if Spartan, surroundings that Smith was to live for the next four years and he was soon engaged in writing his book *Canal Adventures by Moonlight*.

During 1880 Smith had kept badgering friendly MPs about the effects of the new Act besides writing numerous letters to the press on the subject. He managed to arrange for several questions in the House about the implementation of the Act but they elicited only a variety of vague assurances and dusty answers from the President of the Local Government Board. In October Smith wrote to the new Prime Minister but Gladstone merely passed his letter and newspaper cuttings to the appropriate department. This provoking state of affairs continued until early in 1881 when there was an encouraging development. He used the good offices of a friendly MP, Henry Broadhurst, the member for Stoke-on-Trent, a Labour Representative and Secretary to the Trades Union Council, to ask yet another question in the House about the implementation of the Act. Receiving an unsatisfactory answer, Broadhurst saw Dodson, the President of the Local Government Board, in March and, after an equally unsatisfactory interview, told Smith bluntly "that there is nothing for it but to pass an Act making the

Act of 1877 compulsory." He promised that if Smith could get a short Bill drawn up, he would introduce it. Smith was delighted and within twelve days he produced the draft of 'The Canal Boats Act 1877, Amendment Bill' which Broadhurst introduced as a private measure. Based on the criticisms Smith had voiced over the last two years, it sought to remove the permissive element in the original Act. Its intention was four-fold: first, to make the registration of boats compulsory; second, to make efficient inspection of the boats the duty of the Local Government Board; third, to place the education of children under the control of the Local Government Board; and fourth, to prohibit the employment of children and young persons under the age of eighteen on Sundays.

Although the Bill was read a first time on 24 June, it quickly ran into opposition from the canal companies and its progress was blocked first by Sir Edward Watkin and then by Mr. P.A. Taylor. The latter objected to the 'absurd' clause banning Sunday working, while the former, when confronted by Smith in the lobby, loudly declared, "I have blocked the Bill, and intend to block it, and you cannot convert me if you talked for hours on the subject. The children must go without education." The term 'blocking', preventing or postponing the passage of a bill, in this context meant giving notice of opposition to the bill so that it could not be taken after 12.30a.m. Shortly afterwards the Bill was withdrawn without any promise that the Government would bring it in during the next session, and for the time being this was the end of Smith's hopes.

The Government's attitude to the Bill did not go unnoticed by the press. A leading article in *The Weekly Times* on 10th July stated: "I fear, from the state of public business, that the thousands of poor children interested must wait another session before their wants will receive attention". Smith was furious at what had happened and complained bitterly in a letter to the Prime Minister on 10th August: "My many years hard work and expenses have been thrown away, and the education of the canal children put off to an indefinite period." Gladstone replied that he was sure Sir William Harcourt (the Home Secretary) also much regretted the loss of the Canal Boats Amendment Act. It was scant consolation to Smith. He brooded over his failure during his travels in the Midlands until he could contain his anger no longer.

In *The Manchester Guardian* on 29th November, he fulminated:

> I say it with all reason, burning language, logic, and force of conviction I can command, that on and after January 1882, any little boat

child that dies through the apathy of the Government and machinators' wickedness shall be as a little Abel whose blood shall cry from the ground.

Smith returned to his writing. He swiftly brought his *Canal Adventures by Moonlight* up to date and published it in August. Besides including accounts of his winter journey and his boat trip from London to Leicester, it contained much other material in the shape of letters and articles about gypsy children and also details of his efforts to get his Canal Boats Amendment Bill passed. In it Smith often refers to the canal children as his 'Rob Rats'. This is a reference to a book, *Rob Rat: a Story of Barge Life*, by the Rev. Mark Guy Pearse, published in 1879 and dedicated to Smith. Pearse, a Wesleyan minister who later became a friend of Smith's, wrote this sentimental tale about a narrow boat called the *Water Rat* at a time when life on the canals was arousing much interest. Inspired by Smith's work for the children, it proved highly popular, selling over twenty thousand copies.

In his book Pearse quotes passages from *Our Canal Population* and endorses Smith's views on cabins, indecency and ignorance. The boatman (Old Rat) and his wife are the usual drunken, violent stereotypes who make life a misery for their young son, Rob (Rat), and his sister, "lame little Lizer", whose hip was damaged in a fall caused by Old Rat in his cups. The children dream of living on a boat where there is no drinking and no beating. Rob, thrown off the boat by his father in a fit of rage, is rescued by Noah, a saintly old boatman, owner of the *Ark*. Noah, who, it must be said, bears more than a passing resemblance to Smith, teaches Rob to say his prayers and know his Bible. Eventually Rob and lame little Lizer are re-united and their dream is realised on the *Ark*. They determine to repay Noah's kindness by showing kindness to others; the moral of the story is "Pass it on".

Two points emerge from Smith's *Canal Adventures by Moonlight*. The first is how well he is known by boatmen and their families as a result of his numerous visits to canal wharves in the Midlands over the years. He is treated rather roughly and with coarse humour by some boatmen but others appreciated his concern for their welfare and his efforts on behalf of their children. He was always at ease with the children; he delighted in talking to them about Jesus, and his capacious bag was always full of simple reading books, coloured pictures, oranges, sweets and other little trifles for them. He also carried magazines and half-ounce packets of tobacco for the boatmen and their wives to sweeten his way. All these items he paid for himself, as he had always done when in employment, but now the money had to come out of the little he was able to scrape together.

Secondly, it is obvious that in his penniless state he had to depend for all his travelling expenses, including his lodgings and his food, upon the charity of friends and well-wishers. He lived a hand to mouth existence, constantly short of money, sometimes reduced to a couple of coppers in his pocket. On one occasion, when arriving home from London late on a Saturday evening, he found he only had sixpence left to provide food for the following week, and he was forced to sell his gold 'Albert' (watch chain). There are many such references in his diaries during this period to similar crises he encountered on his travels. Yet it is striking how often people came to his rescue when he was in extremis. Many who met this untidy, shabby, poverty-stricken man were impressed by his earnestness and his determination to carry on his work regardless of his empty pockets. We constantly find clerics, businessmen, chance acquaintances and those who had heard something of his work among the poor, quietly helping him with sums ranging from ten shillings to ten pounds and more.

Smith was bitterly disappointed at the failure of his Bill to make progress, but he refused to give up and continued to write letters and send copies of his articles to friends and sympathisers in and out of Parliament. He had precious little to show for it after many months. His only consolation was the £700 he finally received from the fund set up for his benefit two years before. This was a tremendous blessing and made a great difference to his life over the next couple of years. It solved his domestic problems and provided him with the means to carry on his work.

Although still unable to interest leading politicians in re-introducing and supporting his Canal Boats Amendment Bill, a momentary ray of hope broke through the gloom in April, 1883. Thanks chiefly to the good offices of Sir Charles Dilke, the new President of the Local Government Board, and his old ally Mundella, now Vice-President of the Committee of Council on Education, the Canal Boats Act 1877 Amendment Bill was re-introduced and read a first time. Smith was in good spirits once more but his joy was short-lived; when the Bill came up for its second reading, Mr. Salt, the MP for Stafford, blocked it successfully by having it referred to the Select Committee on Canals.

Further blows of a personal nature were to follow. In August a telegram informed him that his mother had died suddenly and peacefully at the age of seventy-two. Then in October there was another attempt to find a post suitable for Smith's talents and experience. Several of his friends, including Lord Derby, Lord Aberdare and Charles Spurgeon, approached Gladstone informally and suggested he should give Smith some appointment in connection with the administration of the Canal Boats Act. Regrettably nothing came of it and Smith had to struggle along as best he could.

That autumn he appeared before the Social Science Congress at Huddersfield to give two papers, one dealing with the Canal Boats Acts and the other with what he called "Our Gypsy, Van and Show Children". He continued to harp on the miseries and dangers of life in the cabins and harrowed up the souls of his audience by thundering "in some instances there will be father and three grown-up daughters sleeping side by side; again, a man, a woman and two young men, sleeping with no partition between them." He paused dramatically. Then, like the Ghost of Hamlet's father who could a tale unfold, he rammed home his message: "I could tell this Congress of things that have taken place in the cabins that would' cause the ears to tingle and the face to turn pale of every England-loving Englishman and woman, if they did but know the facts. I myself shudder to think about them."

Meanwhile, the Select Committee had continued to hold meetings and examine witnesses during the sessions of 1883 and 1884. On 4th July Smith was invited to attend one of them with W.E. Forster, the architect of the seminal Education Act of 1870, in the chair. By now the failings of the 1877 Act had become obvious to the Committee. Enforcement had proved very difficult. The Registration Authorities were not bound to enforce the Act, and the Local Government Board had no powers to make them do so. Thus the regulations issued by the Local Government Board were ignored without fear of penalty. Fresh legislation was imperative.

Smith was rigorously questioned for three and a half hours upon all aspects of what he had said and written in recent years about the plight of the canal children. Smith insisted that no Act could work without the active involvement of central government and that reports by local authorities and compulsory registration would achieve nothing without regular and frequent inspections of boats throughout the canal system. His detailed knowledge of the waterways, his concern for the children and his striking sincerity carried the day. A few days later, early one fine sunny morning, his Canal Boats Amendment Bill passed through the Committee without amendment. Smith, who had been sitting anxiously in the Speaker's Gallery until 3.45 a.m., "could have shouted for joy" but managed to restrain himself. Instead he went out and celebrated with "a coffee stall breakfast for 2½d at Marble Arch". At last, on 14th August, the Bill received the Royal Assent.

The revised Act had the teeth that Smith had long worked for. Registration and Sanitary Authorities had powers to enforce both the Act and the Regulations issued by the LGB, while the Education Department had the duty to see that the children attended school. It was now obligatory for all canal boats to be registered annually and for them to be inspected regularly to ensure cleanliness and to abolish overcrowding.

After six years of persistent writing and lobbying, Smith had finally won the day. It had been a long gruelling struggle and he and his family had suffered much privation during it. Although deeply satisfied at the result, Smith was cautious in his rejoicing. He was enough of a realist to know that the future of the boys and girls on the canals depended upon regular inspections of the boats to ensure the Act was being complied with.

The Act also created the post of Chief Inspector of Canal Boats. This was an attractive position carrying a starting salary of £500 and rising by annual increments to £900, plus expenses, the standard salary given to non-technical Inspectors of the Local Government Board. The press and public fully expected George Smith to be appointed as a result of his endeavours over the years. Certainly there was no man better qualified to oversee the efficient operation of the new Act and Smith would have given his ears for the post. Although he had been given the impression, a nod here, a wink there, that he would be appointed, it went to another. Even as early as 1880 Smith had been considered a most suitable candidate for the post of inspector. In August that year he had written to Major-General Burnaby, MP for North Leicestershire, asking for his help over the operation of the Canal Boats Act. In a reply offering to do all he could, Burnaby added, "I think you would make a good inspector." As Hodder remarked, Smith's was the common fate of pioneers: "One soweth and another reapeth".

The post was first offered to Henry Broadhurst, the Radical MP for Stoke-on-Trent, who was sorely tempted to accept what he considered "an ample salary, a secure position for life and pleasant work." Because of his Parliamentary commitments Broadhurst finally decided against it, a decision he later admitted he regretted. Eventually the post was filled by John Brydone, a Scottish businessman aged forty four, the successful manager of the Stoke Prior Salt Works at Droitwich. Smith was mortified; such a post would have provided the security he had always sought for his wife and family. Vigorous protests on his behalf were made in the press by George

Howell MP and others but to no effect. His case was taken up by a leading article in the *English Independent*:

> Again and again, in public and in private, has the matter been pressed on the attention of Mr. Sclater-Booth. Why has Mr. Smith not been appointed? Have prejudices gathered against the faithful worker during twenty years which have become influential in the Tory upper air? Is Mr. Smith too plebeian? He is an earnest Christian. Can it be that this has blocked his way? Unfortunately, we know only too well what Toryism is. Not thus would it have been had Liberal statesmen been in power.

The autumn was a disheartening time for Smith but he was determined not to be downcast by his lack of advancement. He saw his future role as an acting-unpaid, self-appointed inspector, watching to see if the provisions of the new Act were being properly carried out by those appointed for the purpose. He never wavered in his concern over the future of the children from the brick-yards and the canals, but now that he had two pieces of legislation in place, he found his new crusade on behalf of gypsy and travelling children much more absorbing.

In effect, his work for the boat-children was done. It is fair to say that the Act of 1884 resulted in a rapid and dramatic improvement in living conditions on the boats. Marked progress was made in restricting the number of people occupying the cabins (less 'herding together') and the cabins improved in cleanliness. Most boatmen had the sense to realise the Act was working in their favour and the local authority inspectors were soon seen as friends. There were still the usual evasions by the unscrupulous and there were still dirty boats, but the number steadily decreased over the years as a result of regular inspections.

All these improvements rubbed off on the life of the boat children. With attendance at school being enforced (though not always achieved) by the Education Department, illiteracy sharply declined. Girls over twelve continued to find their way into domestic service and to profit from what they learned there. Boatmen increasingly took homes 'on the bank' and left wife and children behind while they worked their boat with a son or hired hand. Canal life may still have been some way from the idyll suggested by *The Times* but Smith could walk the towpath of the Midlands with a sense of pride in what he had achieved.

Brydone's appointment turned out to be a most successful one. Sensibly, he pursued a path of conciliation and understanding towards the boatmen, refusing to condemn them all for the excesses of a few, a policy Smith strongly supported. Brydone refused to see the boatmen "as a degraded, almost outcast race, but as a useful body of men engaged in an arduous yet honourable calling, helping to carry on with advantage the commerce of the country." Later on, however, Brydone's ideas for improvements and his criticism of various local authorities found little favour with the Local Government Board and soured his relationship with his superiors. One can only imagine what explosions might have occurred if Smith had found himself in conflict with the department. With hindsight, those who opposed Smith's appointment as Chief Inspector were probably right. Even his friends "could not take both the man and his enthusiasm".

Sadly, Brydone, who had done so much to lay the foundation for a thorough and sensible implementation of the Act, died from overwork and illness in 1899 at the age of fifty~eight. He left this tribute to Smith's contribution:

"However mistaken may have been some of his views and however exaggerated may have been some of the statements his enthusiasm led him to make, still to him must be accorded the merit of having aroused the attention of Parliament to the necessity of legislating for the peculiar condition of this people, and thus to him the canal boat population owe a debt of obligation the full benefit of which they do not give him credit for."

There was to be a silver lining for Smith at the end of the year. On the 11th November he received a cheque for £300 from the Royal Bounty Fund for special services. This time it was made on the recommendation of Mr. Gladstone in acknowledgement of Smith's work on behalf of the canal children. By a happy coincidence the cheque arrived on Mary Smith's birthday. Smith and his children had clubbed together to buy her a present, a corset, price three shillings, which they put on the table in front of her after breakfast. Smith then produced the cheque and with a flourish laid it on top. Mary was quite overcome and the family became so excited that they failed to say their morning prayers as reverently as usual.

This gift relieved their immediate needs. Smith's reaction to his unexpected good fortune is typical and inspiring. He wrote in his diary: "To God be all the praise. I've got the Treasury order and I shall spend it in helping the cause of the gypsy children." One simply has to admire the man. Yet Smith's friends in the press and in Parliament felt that something more was required in view of his valiant exertions over the years. It was suggested that a national subscription should be organised to relieve him of financial worries for the rest of his life.

A few days later on 21 November an advertisement appeared in the *Pall Mall Gazette* for a 'George Smith of Coalville Fund' to be set up for the benefit of Smith and his family. This was the work of the editor, W.T. Stead, who had become a good friend of Smith's during the brick-yard days and had been instrumental in publicising his efforts and rallying support among influential politicians and his fellow-editors. Stead wrote: "The reward of philanthropy such as his should not be literal starvation, and men of his disinterested enthusiasm and capacity in philanthropic work should at least be allowed their rations". Stead laid down that every penny subscribed (and he already had many offers of substantial help from those who knew and appreciated Smith's work) should be handed over without any deductions to trustees, who would invest the money on Smith's behalf so that he could enjoy the interest during his lifetime. On his death, the capital would be divided among his children. When the fund was finally closed in October the following year, there was a sum of £1,480 to be invested in "British, Indian or Colonial securities or English Railway debentures".

On the strength of his unexpected windfall from the Royal Bounty and the promise of more to come in the spring from Stead's Fund, Smith's financial problems were at an end. He was able to buy and repair a house he was later to christen The Cabin in the village of Crick, some four and a half miles away. It was a curious house then, consisting of three sixteenth century cottages knocked into one with a gabled roof, huge fireplaces, low ceilings and tiny paned windows. It was here that Smith was to spend the rest of his life. The house still stands in Laud's Lane though it is considerably altered since Smith's time. It is now one of the most imposing houses in the village and has an attractive garden. After Smith's death it was occupied by his son, Grosart, who carried on his medical practice from it. In due course Grosart took a Dr. Morrison into partnership and it was the latter who gave The Cabin its more prestigious name, Queen's House, as befitted its origin. Today, regrettably, it is no longer labelled Queen's House, although older residents still call it that; it is simply 22, Laud's Lane. On the 29th April, Smith records in his diary that he and his family "cleared out of our old stone and thatched house at Welton and began our tramp on a bright spring evening across lovely fields to my new home."

Crick was not so attractive a village as Welton. Hodder, who was rarely unkind about anything or anybody, was certainly unimpressed by it. He contrasted the number of flourishing public houses in the placewith the struggle the church and chapels had to survive there. He ascribed the 'bad

Queen's House, Crick, formerly The Cabin

tone' of the place to the fact that the village once swarmed with navvies "of a very low type" and had never really recovered from the invasion. Smith did not appear unduly troubled about his move; perhaps he saw the village more as a garden full of weeds inviting some vigorous evangelical hoeing. In any case Crick was equally well-suited to his purpose as Welton. The Leicester section of the Grand Union Canal ran close by, while the Oxford and Grand Union Canals were not far away. Although he still remained concerned about the enforcement of the Canal Act, he was now in a position to devote himself whole-heartedly to what was to be his last enthusiasm — the 'travelling children'.

Chapter 13: Bread and Circuses

> The gypsy's life is a joyous life,
> So roving, gay, and free.
>
> Old Song

We must now retrace our steps a little and return to 1879. It was then, when he was already several years into his campaign on behalf of the canal children, that the idea of helping gypsy and other travelling children crystallised in Smith's mind. He had been aware of gypsies and their children since he was a small boy. There was a gypsy encampment on waste land at the back of Peake's Tileries and the ragged, half-starved children he encountered were even more abject than the children working in the brick-yards or on the canal boats. When he was tending the kilns at night, he used to see some of the young ones skulking around the brick-yards looking for unconsidered trifles. He had good reason to remember them. The story goes that he had saved up to buy a book on Natural History, costing five shillings, which he intended to study during the quiet hours at work. The first night he took it into the yard it was stolen by gypsy children. He must have been distressed at the time but many years afterwards he surprisingly records: "This incident later helped to fan my sympathy for the gypsy children into a livelier flame."

He had, of course, come across gypsy families during his working life, but it was only in recent years he had become concerned about their children while visiting narrow boats and walking the canals. What he noticed on his journeys fired him with indignation and aroused his pity. Nomadic, unregulated, Godless, ignorant and dirty, the gypsies appeared to Smith as the outcasts of the Victorian world. As they wandered along the margins of society, their way of life increasingly brought them into conflict with the interests of a settled society. The plight of the children touched his heart. Even though he was already committed to helping the canal children, and would be involved for several years yet, he felt he could no longer ignore the present suffering and the future prospects of the travelling children. He saw them as a fit subject for his endeavours and his concern was soon translated into action.

Smith realised it would be quite possible to run his campaigns for the canal and gypsy children in tandem. He would be able to combine his fact-finding journeys along the canals investigating the operation of the Canal Boats Act with close observation of the gypsy families he encountered on the way. As it turned out, the two worked well together, particularly in the bleak years of 1879 to 1884 when, frustrated by lack of progress with his Canal Boats Amendment Bill, he was able to turn with relief to this other crusade.

It was not simply gypsy children that Smith wanted to help. He made it clear that he wanted to improve the living conditions and bring the benefits of education to all those he termed 'travelling children'. Today we use the emollient but pejorative term 'travellers' to denote a motley group of individuals and families, including gypsies, New Age travellers and others who live on the road. This was not so in Smith's day. By 'travelling children' Smith meant the children of the travelling population who lived in a variety of temporary homes such as vans, carts, handcarts, and tents. The great majority, of course, were gypsies but there were also the children of those working as 'showmen' in fairs, and of those involved in circuses and menageries, as well as the offspring of tinkers, vagrants and those unemployed couples actively seeking work. We shall say something about each of these groups in turn.

Since the gypsies figure so largely in Smith's campaign and his later years, it will be helpful to examine briefly their background, how they lived and how they were regarded at this time by the public, factors which governed the condition and treatment of their children about whom Smith was so concerned. It is now generally accepted that the gypsies originally came from Northern India some one thousand years ago and over the centuries spread through Asia Minor into Greece and thence into Europe, arriving in England and Scotland in the sixteenth century. Others came through Egypt (hence 'Egyptians' and thus 'gypsies'), spread along the North African coast and penetrated Spain. Aloof and secretive, the gypsies preserved much of their racial and cultural identity. They spoke Romani, a corrupt dialect of Hindi with a large admixture of words from various European languages, and referred to themselves as Romani.

In Smith's day they made a curious and fitful living from horse-dealing (at which they were highly skilled), knife-grinding, tinkering pots and pans, mending chair bottoms and making pegs and baskets. Their wives hawked these round villages and towns, as well as selling on other items such as flowers and mats bought in the markets. The women were skilled beggars

George Smith handing out sweets near Latimer Road, Notting Dale, London (1879)

and came into their own as importunate fortune tellers when the families attended fairs and race-meetings.

Smith's main pre-occupation was their living conditions on the roads in summer and in their winter quarters. He describes meeting a band of gypsies on the road:

> A motley crowd of half-naked savages, carrion eaters, dressed in rags and tatters, and shreds, usually called men and women — some running, walking, loitering, traipsing, shouting, gaping and staring: the women with children on their backs and in their arms; old men and women tottering along; hordes of children following in the rear; hulking men, with lurcher dogs at their heels, sauntering along in idleness, spotting out their prey; donkeys loaded with sacks, mules with tents and sticks, and their vans and wagons carrying ill-gotten gains and plunder.

He gives details of their caravans (never called such by the Romani, always a 'vardo' or living wagon) and the tents and carts used by many gypsy families. Because the nature of these 'movable dwellings' may be unfamiliar, I have quoted his descriptions of several of them — and what he found inside. Many of the poorer gypsy families lived in various types of cart, roughly covered over. At Oxford, during St. Giles Fair, he found:

Upon a tumble-down donkey-cart covered over with sticks and old sheeting, drawn by a donkey in harness not worth sixpence, which was tied together with string and pieces of rope, there were women and six poor half-dressed, half-starved, dirty, ragged children. The sight was most pitiable. The little dirty faces, with matted hair, peering through an opening in the rotten calico, reminded me of a nest of young rabbits.

At Long Buckby:

There stood what, so far as the underworks indicated, had been once an old fish-cart, over the top of which had been placed some half-barrel hoops, covered with old tarpaulin sheets. The outside woodwork consisted of pieces of orange boxes, packing cases etc. and was daubed over with paint little better than a child would daub a pigsty door. Inside the van, on the doorsteps, and upon the shafts of their old tumbledown cart, there were man, woman and five-children. The rags of bedding were grimy, greasy and dirty to the last degree. In the midst of this dirt and filth the father was stirring 'rock' which was boiling in an old saucepan upon a little six-inch square stove. This precious dainty, composed of flour, sugar, treacle and grease was to be dealt out by his wife and children by halfpenny-worths at fairs, feasts and races. For a whole month during the winter, they had pushed their van about Lincolnshire in the dark, because they had no horse and they presented too wretched a spectacle for daylight travelling.

Smith found a family with even more primitive arrangements at Daventry:

Gypsy quarters, Plaistow Marshes

Encampment at Mitcham Common

> Connected with one of the 'Aunt Sally' establishments there were a man, woman and three little neglected children, with no other sleeping accommodation than a 'bottom' of straw spread under the stall, covered with an old sheet, and warmed in the winter with an old oil lamp. It was a picture of poverty, despair, degradation and misery. Their stall and 'Aunt Sally' were pushed through the country on a small hand-cart.

Other poor families lived in shocking squalor in primitive tents (Smith calls the cruder ones 'wigwams') of all shapes and sizes pitched on the bare earth.

In Essex he tracked down a small colony of gypsies and making his way through thick mud he came upon "a bulky, dirty, greasy, idle-looking fellow, who might never have been washed in his life", lounging on a broken chair outside a tent. Inside were:

> five children as ragged as wild goats, as filthy as pigs, and quite as ignorant. On an old 'squab bed' — the only bed in the room — sat a big, fat, aged gypsy woman. A young gypsy of about eighteen years stood at the bottom of the bed enjoying his Sunday dinner, a kind of mixture of meat, soup, fish, broth, roast and fry, thickened with bones and flavoured with snails and bread. In one hand he held the plate, and the other had to do duty in place of a knife and fork. Upon a very rickety stool sat a girl with a dirty bare bosom suckling a poor emaciated baby, whose father nobody seemed to know — and if report be true — the less said about paternity the better. In this one little hole with a floor covered with dirt and mud about half an inch thick, one bed teeming with vermin, and walls covered with greasy grime, this family lived and slept.

In London Smith visited an encampment at Cherry Island and found about thirty tents in which there were "between one and two hundred gypsy children growing up worse than Zulus". He describes one of the larger and better equipped tents:

> It is about seven feet wide, sixteen feet long, and where the round top is highest, is about four feet and a half in height. It is covered with old pieces of canvas or sacking to keep out the cold and rain, and the entrance is closed with a kind of curtain; the fire by which they cook their meals is placed in a tin bucket pierced with holes and the smoke goes out of an opening at the top of the tent. The bed is a little straw laid on the damp ground, covered with a sack or sheet; an old soap-box or tea-chest serves both as cupboard and table. Here they live, father and mother, brothers and sisters, huddled up together.

Smith soon found that the poorer gypsies did not use plates or dishes or cutlery. Their kitchen equipment consisted simply of an earthenware pot and an iron pan from which nearly all of them ate with their fingers. Better-class gypsies had a jug or basin to serve out whatever they were boiling upon their fire, but few had any crockery.

The children of the many gypsies who had their own vans fared much better. Smith admits that, as in the case of the canal boatmen and their wives, he met many gypsy families who kept tolerably clean vans and cared for their numerous children. Admittedly their living quarters were cramped, but this was infinitely preferable to sleeping on vermin-infested straw under a cart or in the trodden mud of a primitive tent.

Smith was a man of his time; much as he deplored the condition and fate of the gypsy children he shared the popular prejudices (sadly, generally justified) towards the adult Romani. Smith's attitude stemmed from what he had observed on the road and in their encampments where their dwellings were as filthy and repulsive as the cabins of narrow boats. In them, children were born, suffered from disease, died and were hastily buried by the roadside. The survivors grew up in dirt and ignorance, ragged and unwashed, to quarrel and fight, to poach and steal and become the terror of the neighbourhood wherever their caravans rested. The gypsies, he wrote, practise "lying, begging, thieving, cheating, and every other abominable low and cunning craft, backed by ignorance and idleness. In many instances, they live like pigs and die like dogs". A latent hostility towards the gypsy still exists today but in fairness to our contemporary Romani, I must stress that I am dealing with the popular view of them in the nineteenth century.

The gypsies did not spend all their time travelling. When they felt the first chill winds of winter and the pleasures and profits of country life declined, the gypsies made for London and the large towns and sought the relative comfort of winter quarters. They usually settled in the yards of public houses, in disused brick-fields, on marshes, commons and pieces of waste ground; these were traditional sites to which they returned year after year. Liverpool, for example, was full of camping grounds on the open heathlands around the city, such as Walton, Tranmere, Green Lane and Waverton Fields. Not many miles away, Earlestown and Newton-le-Willows also harboured gypsy communities in the winter. On average, gypsies spent seven months on the roads and five months in winter quarters. Because of this pattern, Smith was able to visit the same families regularly when he was staying in London for long periods. He chose Sundays to go and see them because this was when they were usually found at home, and he recorded a vast number of these visits in his diaries.

Gypsies were often lumped together with tinkers whom they tended to look down upon. The tinkers resembled them in their way of life and in some of their occupations such as tinsmithing and horse-coping, but they were actually a separate race from Ireland with a cryptic language of their own known as Shelta. This language consisted partly of Irish or Gaelic words, disguised by inversion or alteration of initial consonants. True tinkers were not to be confused with feckless Irishmen who had simply taken a fancy to a life on the road. In our context, however, their number is negligible.

After the gypsies, the next largest group of travellers consisted of 'showmen' or fairground operators. It is not generally appreciated that during the first half of the nineteenth century 'showmanship' was a major industry, employing thousands of men and women in fairs, travelling menageries and circuses, all journeying from fair to fair throughout Great Britain. Although there were theatres in the larger cities, the fair was the chief means of entertainment for most people before the coming of the music halls. Fairs were immensely popular, especially in the country where they were often organised to coincide with quarter-days and the hiring of labour. There was a traditional fairground circuit which started on 6 March at Wrexham and ended after the Sheffield Wakes on 28 November; fairs were often held annually on the same day in many towns and villages.

The word 'show' may be defined as any activity that takes place in a booth and attracts a crowd. There were four classes of show. The most important were circuses and menageries. Circuses operated rather differently from the other fairground operators. Instead of moving out after a few days, they tended to stay on in the larger towns and villages for two or three weeks and some eventually found permanent buildings. Circus folk were quite distinct from showmen. Artistes did not mix, even with the more affluent showmen, so there was little social contact and virtually no intermarrying. Travelling menageries were similar in several respects to circuses.

We are indebted to Dickens for much background detail about urban and rural life in the early and middle years of the century. He paints an amusing picture of a travelling circus in *Hard Times* (1854) where Sleary's Circus or Horse-Riding featured the daring vaulting act of Mr. E.W.B.

'The Little Azella' (1868)

Childer, the 'Wild Huntsman of the North American Prairies'. The ladies of the company provided, apparently with the aid of more than one partner, a troupe of small children who "did the fairy business". Small chance there of gaining education on the hoof.

Like other travelling children, those in the circus tended to follow their parents' occupation and specialities. They were considered by Victorian philanthropists to be particularly vulnerable, even though girl gymnasts could earn large sums of money. The eccentric Arthur Munby, that assiduous recorder of the lives of Victorian working women, investigated female gymnasts and in 1868 he noted the exploits of 'The Little Azella', the star attraction of the Holborn Amphitheatre. He met her elder sister there and learned that Azella was a nine year old whose real name was Betsy Asher. Together they watched Betsy's performance on the trapeze with her partner, 'M. de Vigne', to whom she had recently been apprenticed. Munby asked:

> And your little sister really likes to climb and tumble about in this way, like a lad?"
>
> "Well, I only know she says so; and she practises hard enough!"

A young acrobat: Lulu (1871)

"'Does she like that?' I asked; for just then the little Betsy, who was balancing on the trapeze, flung herself boldly off, as if taking a header, and swept head downwards along the inverted body of her master, who was hanging by his heels. He caught her in her descent, by the ankles, and so she hung, head downwards. "Does she like that?" "Yes", said Miss Asher, emphatically and gravely: "she says that's one of the prettiest tricks of all". And she looked calmly at little Betsy hanging so, in her tights and spangles.

Despite the success of the little Azella, the training demands on young circus riders and gymnasts and their introduction into public performances at an early age led to unacceptable physical risks. The problem was drawn to the attention of Lord Shaftesbury who stole a little of Smith's thunder by introducing the Children's Dangerous Performance Act of 1870. This provided that any person causing a child under the age of fourteen to take part in a public performance endangering life and limb could be faced with a fine of up to £10. If the child happened to suffer actual bodily harm in doing so, then the employer would have to pay compensation of up to £20 to the young performer.

Later on, the 'rides' became more important than either the circus or the menagerie. In 1865 S.G. Soame exhibited the first steam-driven roundabout and revolutionised the economics of the fairground. Within ten years the old type of roundabout propelled by a man or a horse disappeared and the large steam-driven ride became the main attraction of the fair. By 1870 Frederick Savage had developed the centre-truck, with the steam engine mounted on a spring truck in the centre of the ride, and was busy supplying them to those showmen who could afford the considerable cost. Rides grew in variety and popularity and ushered in the golden age of fairgrounds which lasted until the outbreak of the Great War.

Next in order were those shows comprising a large tent with pay booth offering such attractions as boxlng, wrestling, and waxworks. They also exhibited unpleasant animal freaks — beasts with six legs or two heads — and a variety of human curiosities including giants, dwarfs, living skeletons, Hottentots, (the proprietor's small children blacked up), pigfaced women and bearded ladies.

Then came the stalls, very much the poor relation of the fair, being mainly gaming tables where the 'flatties' (the fairground name for punters or non-fairground people) tried their luck at the wheel of fortune, quoit-throwing and roll-a-penny. The traditional games of skill, such as darts, rifle-shooting and coconut shies, which could be played against the back canvas of an open stall were also available.

The fourth class of show was a very humble one indeed, barely qualifying for the title of show. It was composed of a small army of freelance operators, carrying their sparse equipment on their backs: clowns, jugglers, thimble-riggers (three thimbles and a pea, a variant of the old three-card trick), peepshows, and Punch and Judy men.

In *The Old Curiosity Shop* (1840-41) Dickens offers us an interesting selection of show-people. It ranges from the prestigious 'Jarley's Wax-works' (proprietor, Mrs. Jarley), for whom Little Nell worked for a time giving a running commentary on the various figures, to Sweet William and his card tricks. We also meet Codlin and Short, the Punch and Judy men, Grinder's stilt-walkers and Jerry, the proprietor of a troupe of dancing dogs. Finally there was Vuffin, who showed a giant and a little lady minus legs and

Little Nell at Mrs. Jarley's Waxworks
(The Old Curiosity Shop)

Jerry and his dancing dogs (The Old Curiosity Shop)

arms. Nell lived in Mrs. Jarley's caravan and Dickens was the first novelist to describe a vardo in detail. Mrs. Jarley's caravan was a very superior vehicle arousing in the reader visions of romantic rural rides, but worlds away from the vardos that Smith came across.

We are fortunate in having a fascinating, if highly-coloured, account of the life led by itinerant fairground children. 'Lord' George Sanger (1827–1911) in his *Seventy Years a Showman* paints a vivid picture of his childhood on the road, featuring body-snatchers, Chartist rioters, fires and fights among showmen. Written with considerable brio, his book emphasises how the children were expected to help their parents in the fairground from early childhood and were regarded as a source of cheap labour. They could only attend school when they were in winter quarters and not too many chose to do so. But they did acquire certain skills. They acted as junior barkers, shouting out to attract the attention of the crowd, and supplying the patter for the peepshows and other delights. The girls learned to handle money while the boys gained useful experience in painting, carpentry and in working with machinery, as well as acquiring one or two other dubious skills. Thus they received a form of practical education on the lower slopes of the University of Life. This was also the case with the offspring of those travelling hawkers and auctioneers who lived in vans.

Some confusion arose during the century about the roles of the gypsies and the showmen. The public formed the impression that gypsies were showmen and that most showmen were gypsies. This was a misunderstanding. The showmen proper always kept themselves apart from the gypsies, who invariably camped in a different spot from that occupied by the showmen's vans and tents. The gypsies were never showmen, though they were sometimes the proprietors of quite large drinking and dancing booths. They inhabited an entirely separate world, similar to that of the showmen only in that it was nomadic. They travelled from fair to fair but they went as horse-dealers, hawkers of baskets and tinware, fortune-tellers and owners of knife and snuff-box shies. These latter were the predecessors of our coconut shies since coconuts were very expensive until late in the century. In this early version small baskets were firmly placed on tall ash rods stuck into the ground against a canvas backcloth. Customers threw large sticks known as livetts at them for two shies a penny. If a basket was dislodged (which was not often) the customer received the prize inside it, usually a cheap knife, tobacco, a snuff box, or a box full of halfpennies. I suppose it could be argued that the shies were technically a show, but this is hardly enough to turn gypsies into showmen,

The last group of travellers' children is a very small one, consisting of the children of a variety of other itinerants including the peripatetic unemployed, vagrants, idlers and the like. A journalist friend of Smith's visited a typical loafer's camp. He found that they had virtually no skills of any kind, except that of shaving skewers which they sold to butchers and fishmongers at tenpence or a shilling a stone. The men lounged about their camp, amusing themselves cooking unsavoury pieces of meat, while the women, rather like their gypsy counterparts, hawked mats and flowers bought on market days. The plight of the children can only be imagined.

Such were the backgrounds of the various types of travelling children on whose behalf George Smith now began his agitation. Having already acquired enough preliminary information for his purpose, Smith announced his intention to improve conditions for gypsy children in a letter to the press. The response was not encouraging. The press thought it was a campaign too far. They reckoned Smith had undertaken a hopeless task, since people held strong views about gypsies and other types of traveller and were indifferent to appeals on their behalf. They also pointed to the small but articulate number of intellectuals who fostered a romantic view of the gypsies' nomadic life and would be opposed to interference with their traditional ways.

This group was a reflection of the growing interest during the middle

George Smith visiting Gypsy children near London

years of the century in gypsy life in general, stemming from the novels of George Borrow and encouraged by the publication (1853) of Matthew Arnold's *The Scholar Gypsy*. It resulted in the formation in 1880 of the Gypsy Lore Society by a number of 'Romanophiles' or 'gypsophilists'. The Society's activities revolved round research into Romani lore and language. Their journals barely touched upon the contemporary problems of the Romani in England and certainly not on the condition of their children. The Society foundered through lack of interest in 1892.

Smith refused to be discouraged by such a depressing forecast and he started off full of confidence. He decided to concentrate on the most numerous group, the gypsy boys and girls, and his first task was to build up a dossier about the conditions under which they lived. He visited many gypsy encampments and the fairs, markets and race meetings where they might be found, recording his impressions and the results of his interviews in detail as he went. If it was difficult to estimate the canal population, Smith found it even more difficult to put a figure on the number of gypsy children living in the country, mainly because of the Romani's dislike of the census and their successful efforts to evade it. Smith's figure of 50,000, which he seems to have plucked out of the air, is a considerable exaggeration; the census of 1891 gives a total of 13,000 which is almost certainly an understatement.

Smith quickly acquired a mass of material which he spent much of the winter months shaping into what he hoped would prove a compelling and emotive account of the gypsy problem. He naturally kept Queen Victoria *au fait* with his progress. One of his more interesting diary entries runs thus:

Writing long letter to the Queen, enclosing cuttings etc. Before sealing it up I placed it upon my chair, and knelt down before it, and said, "Lord, bless the letter, and may it do good in moving hearts at headquarters to come to the help of the poor gypsy children.

In addition to letters and articles in the press, Smith again chose the Social Science Congress in October for the promulgation of his views. He secured the necessary invitation to Manchester where he read a paper on the condition of the gypsy and other travelling children under the title of 'The Cry of the Gypsy Children and our Roadside Arabs'. The very word 'gypsy' sent a frisson of excitement down the spines of his audience. It conjured up visions of a nomadic and exotic life full of eastern promise, a far cry from Smith's usual wretched world of brick-yards and canals. But the frissons were short-lived and the visions proved a mirage. His paper turned out to contain rather more of the same. In it he deplored the fact that so many of the Romani men and women were unmarried, though he was unable to furnish any reliable figures. He emphasised the large size of the families he had come across and the fact that very few gypsies could read or write. He felt that the children, as well as being illiterate, were already following in the devious footsteps of their parents and were well on their way to self-destruction. He ended by outlining his plans for reform. Arguing that boatmen and gypsies were both nomads and shared similar problems, he based his proposals closely upon the provisions of his recent Canal Boats legislation.

In the summer of 1880 Smith published the fruits of his labours and travels in a book entitled *Gypsy Life; being an account of our Gypsies and their children. With suggestions for their improvement.* Smith prided himself on his attempt to show at considerable length the reasons for, and the probable date of, the gypsies leaving India and the route by which they eventually reached Europe. He also went into much detail about the reasons for their persecution after their arrival in England from the Continent and about their present condition. His material was not the result of any original research but simply achieved by copying out lengthy sections from books, reviews, and magazine articles on the subject. These were flung together, to form an ill-digested mass of historical fact and speculation.

When speaking for himself, Smith was at pains to strip away the spurious glamour of gypsy life. He dismissed fortune-telling, palmistry and sorcery and he confessed he could see neither charm in fraud nor romance in thieving. His book is based on the assumption, as Hodder puts it,"that a genuine Englishman hates the man who will not work, despises the man who will cheat and lie, and is vigilant to keep within reach of the arm of the law all crafty and subtle impostors". What comes across most strongly in the book is Smith's passionate concern about the children fated to live in physical and moral squalor and in danger of acquiring the mysterious occupations of their parents.

At least one reviewer of *Gypsy Life* supported Smith's harsh view of the Romani and derided those whose "romantic imagination pictures the gypsy as a sort of peripatetic philosopher, with more of Jacques in him than Autolycus: living in constant communication with nature, sleeping in the open air, subsisting on the scantiest food, slaking his thirst at the running brook, and only begging to be allowed to live his own childlike and innocent life. Aesthetic enthusiasm of this kind is apt to be severely checked by the prosaic realities of actual existence.

But the book was not enthusiastically received. It failed to engage the sympathies either of the public or of those MPs who had previously supported Smith and it made little impact compared with his books about the brick-yard and canal children. It did at least provide him with material for his future books on the subject for, as usual, Smith recycled his material unblushingly in an attempt to maintain the momentum of his campaign. Unfortunately, his championship of the travelling children was to prove something of an anti-climax to his career as a reformer.

Chapter 14: The Romany Rye

> Hope deferred maketh the heart sick.
> *Proverbs*

But for the moment Smith pressed on undeterred. At the end of September, 1880 he packed his Gladstone bag and caught the train into Leicester. He visited the Leicester Races before taking the train to Edinburgh where the Social Science Congress for that year was being held. On the first of October he read two papers, the one that concerns us here being entitled, "The Inspection of Gipsy Tents, Habitable Vans, and other Temporary Dwellings". This turned out to be something of a mis-nomer because his paper focused on the education of the gypsy children. However, his paper did end with a detailed statement of his general plans for reform. The ideas that Smith had floated in his paper the previous year at Manchester had now become firm proposals and they were to remain the basis of his legislative plans.

They were based on the three principles of registration, sanitation and education. Thus all movable and temporary dwellings were to be registered by means of a certificate, renewable annually and costing ten shillings, under which the number, age and sex of the van occupants would be regulated. Smith had no wish to hound the gypsy families but he did want their squalid living conditions to be improved and he advocated bringing their dwellings under the inspection of sanitary officers.

Above all, Smith wanted the travelling children brought under the Education Code which would involve compulsory school attendance for a minimum number of days. He suggested that each travelling pupil should be provided with an educational pass book to be presented to, and certified by, the school teacher who, for his pains, would receive one penny per attendance per pupil. This was at best only a very partial solution to the problem and one that was to find little favour with those wielding power either inside or outside Parliament. Smith had come up against a formidable problem, though at this time he does not seem to have realised quite how formidable it was to prove.

If gypsy and other travelling children were to be educated, then regular attendance at school was necessary. The only way this could be properly achieved and enforced would involve gypsy families giving up their nomadic life, settling down and finding work in the community into which Smith hoped, they would be absorbed. To this end he recommended that plots of waste land should be made available for leasing cheaply to gypsies as an incentive to settle down. This logical and seemingly simple solution to the education problem was, of course, in direct conflict with the view that gypsies were members of an ancient scattered race with the right to preserve their cherished nomadic way of life. Many gypsies jealously guarded their heritage. It is worth noting in passing that this problem over the gypsies' place and future in a modern society remains with us today though in a much modified form. The gypsies contrive to live apart from the mainstream, occasionally finding themselves at odds with wary householders. They still shun the idea of becoming wage-earners, preferring the independence offered by their traditional employments. And they continue to represent the idea of liberating romance to those pent up in towns and suffocated by the suburbs.

As for enforcement, qualified sanitary officers, School Board visitors, inspectors, or government officials were to be empowered to enter (and detain, if necessary) tents, vans, shows or other movable or temporary dwellings at any time to check that the law was being properly carried out. There were to be one or two main revisions made during the following years but his main proposals remained substantially unchanged.

It says much for Smith's kindly personality and patent sincerity during his travels and visits that he was able to win the support of a number of senior gypsy families for his plans to improve their living conditions and give their children the chance of a basic education. He had the gift of being able to talk simply and from the heart to all sorts and conditions of men and women, and the gypsies were left in no doubt of his good intentions towards them. At first it seems that the gypsy families supported his proposals, even the annual registration fee of ten shillings, although it is not clear to what extent they understood the implications. However, occupied as he was with the passage of the Canal Boats Amendment Bill, it was to be a long time before his legislative plans were laid before the House.

Throughout 1881 and 1882 Smith continued to fight on two fronts. While he was in lodgings in London overseeing the wearisome and tortuous progress of his Canal Boats Amendment Bill, he took every opportunity to visit and revisit many of the established gypsy sites in and around the capital.

There were 'gypsyries' at Wanstead Flats, Barking, Canning Town, Hackney Flats, Hackney Marshes, Battersea, Wandsworth, Chelsea, Notting Hill, Plaistow Marshes and at Cherry Island in West Ham. It was estimated that at this time between fifteen hundred and two thousand gypsies lived in the London area and Smith recorded hundreds of the visits he made in his diaries.

During the dog days of 1882 he shrugged off his disappointment over the lack of parliamentary progress and began a series of visits to places and occasions where gypsies might be found. Smith started off on Easter Monday by visiting gypsies at Loughton and Epping Forest and then attending the Gypsy Fair at Wanstead Flats the following day. He later went to race-meetings at Northampton and Warwick, and to fairs at Boughton Green near Northampton, Hinckley, Daventry, and Banbury, and to the great St. Giles Fair at Oxford. Smith made detailed notes on all he saw during his 'rambles', as he called them, and, encouraged by the success of his *Canal Adventures by Moonlight* published the previous year, began to work them up into a book during the winter.

In September Smith appeared once more at the annual Social Science Congress, this time held at the University College, Nottingham, under the banner of the Health Department. Smith gave two papers, only the second of which concerns us here. It was called "The Conditions of our Gypsies and their Children, with Remedies" and was presented to a distinguished audience including MPs, Factory Inspectors, Medical Officers of Health and officers of the Association. They gazed up at this old man standing there with his white hair down to his shoulders and wearing a luxuriant beard and whiskers. His reputation for colourful invective and erratic behaviour had gone before him and they were unsure what to expect. With a rare flash of self-awareness, Smith commented, "No doubt with my papers, Gladstone bag, spectacles, etc. I presented very much the appearance of 'Mrs. Gamp' at her speechifying table". He then proceeded to let fly. In previous letters and papers Smith had dealt briefly with the conditions and characteristics of the gypsy families but this was the first public occasion on which he attempted to dispel the colour and romance that still surrounded the gypsy in the imagination of some of the public. Smith did not mince his words; the memory of what he had seen during his rambles in the spring and summer was still fresh in his mind: "The gypsies have been, and still are, a disgrace to Christian civilization, leading the lives of vagabonds and demoralising all they have been brought in contact with, by their lying, plundering, dirty, filthy, cheating and crafty habits. Of course, there are exceptions among them and I wish from the bottom of my heart that there were more. They live huddled together regardless of either sex, age or decency, under hedges, in tents, barns, or on the roadside, with but little regard for marriage ceremonies. Their food, in many instances, is little better than garbage or refuse, and the most riff-raff of them bed themselves upon rotten straw."

Smith declared that the colourful, dashing gypsy of novels and romance had died long ago and that today they were no better than ignorant, idle tramps, scamps and vagabonds. The cause of their degradation he generously ascribed to "Christian apathy, legislative indifference, social deadness and philanthropic neglect". Smith made the point that the Church appeared to consider native children in Africa more interesting and deserving than our own half-starved and neglected children at home. Thus Christian aid took "the form of moral pocket handkerchiefs and flannel waistcoats for little negroes in the tropics." What was wanted, he thundered, was not limp-wristed missionary work (another one in the short ribs for the Church of England!) but social, sanitary and educational legislation. And he intended to provide it.

His last journey of the year, and by far the longest and most arduous, was to Kirk Yetholme near Kelso on the Scottish border. He left Leicester on 19th December in six inches of snow and after a bitterly cold and cheerless train journey he eventually reached his destination to find it blanketed in even deeper snow. Gypsies had been known in Scotland since the sixteenth century and Kirk Yetholme was of particular interest to him. This was an old-established gypsy colony where the Romani lived in a row of cottages some half a mile from the village of Town Yetholme. It was the scene of an experiment from the 1830s onwards when John Baird, a minister of the Church of Scotland, tried to persuade the adults to give up travelling and keep their children in the settlement throughout the year so they could go to school and receive religious instruction. Received with modified rapture, his scheme eventually achieved some success and by the time of Smith's visit nearly all the Yetholme gypsies had given up wandering. Yet they still remained, according to Slater's Directory of 1882, "distinguished by peculiarity of habits from the general body of the community". These peculiar habits had been succinctly described twenty years earlier by Dr. Baird in his *Memoir of the Rev. John Baird* as the not unfamiliar ones of "poaching, thieving and blackguardism".

While at Yetholme Smith heard a story underlining the savage conditions the gypsies suffered in winter. He met a friend who had told him that he had been in the hairdresser's recently when "a poor, half-frozen, half-naked, Scotch gypsy girl, with dishevelled hair, came with a small tin can in her hand, begging with tears in her eyes for some hot water". When asked why she wanted it, the girl replied, "My mother's hair is frozen to the ground and I want a little hot water to loosen it".

Smith's account of his travels among the Romani was finished early in 1883 and it was published in May under the title of *I've been A-Gypsying or Rambles among our gipsies and their children in their tents and vans.* As was his custom, he sent a letter to Queen Victoria with a brief covering letter. He received the customary brief but gracious acknowledgement from General Sir Henry Ponsonby, the Queen's private secretary, which he pasted up in his black book as evidence of the continuing interest of Her Majesty in his work. Mr. Gladstone also received a copy, as did many members of the Lords and Commons, editors of the leading national and provincial papers, friends and supporters. The book sold well but it became increasingly apparent that gypsy children did not enjoy the sympathy the public extended to those children exploited in the brick-yards and on the canals.

Although some of the material in his new book had already appeared in *Gypsy Life, I've Been A-Gypsying* is a vastly more satisfactory and engaging work. It is a fascinating account of Smith's encounters with gypsy and quasi-gypsy families at fairs, race-meetings and encampments in England and Scotland. It is a mine of information about their dwellings, their way of life on the road, food, activities and characteristics, and gives an insight into the conditions under which the children grew up.

Smith ran across some curious characters in his travels. One was simply called 'Scare' and when Smith asked him if he had ever been to church since he ran away from home, Scare replied, "No, except when I went with my old woman to be wed, and, thank God, I can show the marriage lines; 'taint many gypsies can show their marriage lines, I can tell you. I haven't been in church or chapel 'cept for then for nearly fifty year." When Smith asked him if he ever prayed, Scare said, "No, but I swears thousands of times. Mother prays for me, and that has to do; she's a good old critter is mother."

At a fair he met a 'fire-king' and asked him how he liked his work:

"At first it was dreadful to get used to the taste of the paraffin and oil. After you've put the blazing fusees* into your mouth, they leave a taste that

---

* A kind of match with a large head of combustible material. O.E.D.

doesn't mix well with your food. If you keep your mouth wet, have plenty of courage, and breathe out freely, the blazing fire won't hurt you. But paraffin's a good thing for the rheumatics. I never have them now."

Smith was shown how to cook hedgehogs and snails, watched the Romani preying on unsuspecting "gorgios" (the Romany name for non-Romani) and learned some of the secrets of horse-trading and horse-doctoring. He wandered about the fairs and race-courses distributing his picture-cards, little books and gifts to old and young, and talking to the gypsy families about his plans to improve their lot. He gives us valuable descriptions of the "shows" at the fairs — boxing booths, coconut shies, Aunt Sallys, mock auctions, shooting galleries — and the stomach-churning refreshments available. Yet the emphasis remains throughout on the gypsy children and the effect this life-style had upon their health and character.

A curious feature of Smith's thinking and fantasising which finds its way into his writings is his love of aphorisms, those principles or precepts pithily expressed. It was his habit, when walking long distances alone, to stop and write down in his notebook the thoughts coursing through his mind. It was also during his "midnight tossings, nocturnal wanderings, and rambles in wonderland" that these "rough and crude gems", as he puts it, came unbidden to his mind and disturbed his sleep. We find occasional entries in his diaries such as: "Could not sleep; rose and aphorised". Many of his aphorisms contain echoes from the Bible while in others the words and imagery reflect his experience of life in the brick-fields and on the canal. There are hundreds of these aphorisms scattered through his diaries and he was given to including dozens in his published works. There are several pages of them in *I've Been A-Gypsying* where they suddenly confront you slap in the middle of the narrative. In many there is an element of amusing freshness and novelty and I have selected a few which underline his attitude to the dangers of drink, certain sins, and ineffective back-sliding clergy:

> Children go astray when parents leave the gate open, or when the household fence is out of order. The devil plays most with those he means to bite the hardest. A publican's cellar is the storehouse of sorrows. The best stimulating food for an overworked brain is the essence of Divine love, and grace and truth in equal quantities, to be taken upon the knees as often as circumstances need. Before applying to the Great Physician for this medicine, the patient should spend an hour in meditation and solitude. A Christian minister who preaches science instead of Christianity and the Bible, is going through a dark tunnel with a dim lamp

at the end of his boat. A gin-shop is the devil's headquarters, with the landlord as his recruiting sergeant, and rags as the standard colours of his army. Those who dabble in sin stain their hands with indelible ink, which nothing but grace can remove. Prayer is a pump-handle, and faith the rods and bucket that lift the clear spring of heavenly truth into our earthly vessels to refresh us on the way to Zion. Gypsies, vagrants, tramps and vagabonds are the corns and bunions of society. Christians who have to live in, and wade through, the mud of slander and lying pools of deceit have need to wear watertight boots.

It is interesting to see the way he heightens his written message with homespun expressions, rather like his father. Two examples will suffice:

It does appear that the world would have been better if some professing Christians had been pickled like walnuts, when young and green; as it is, they have become hard to crack, and troublesome to handle and rotten within. Some Christians, like bullocks, require rails to be hung upon their necks, to keep them from jumping the fences.

In the previous November Smith had urged his friend, Thomas Burt MP, to put a question to the government about the education of gypsy children in the hope of eliciting a promise of early legislation or at least of stirring them into some kind of response. Rebuffed but undeterred, Smith tried another tack in 1883. He attempted to have a clause inserted in his Canal Boats Act Amendment Bill then before the House (for the third time!) to include gypsy and other travelling children as well as the main beneficiaries, the canal children. Again he was disappointed. Neither Sir Charles Dilke, President of the Local Government Board, nor Mundella, were inclined to muddy the waters with what would undoubtedly have proved a contentious issue.

It was the start of a series of disappointments for Smith that would stretch over the next decade and prove an elongated anti-climax to his career as a reformer. His failure to carry through any kind of measure reduced him at times almost to despair and he was to die with success in his third campaign still eluding him. It would be wearisome to dwell in detail on the shifts and devices he employed, the hopes quickly raised and as quickly dashed, and the opposition to his proposals in the House of Commons. It will be sufficient for our purposes to consider briefly the fate of those bills appearing before the House under various titles but with the same unwavering purpose. The more Smith's frustration grew, the more stubborn and determined he became to ensure that the less acceptable clauses of his bills were passed. He would brook no compromise and his friends shook their heads behind his back and were saddened by his rejection of the art of the possible.

In 1884 he was asked by Sir Charles Dilke, Chairman of the Royal Commission on the Housing of the Poor, to give evidence before it about the condition of the gypsies, on which he was now regarded as something of an expert. He found himself faced by a powerful group, including the Marquis of Salisbury, Sir Richard Cross (the former Home Secretary) and Cardinal Manning. They questioned him closely for about half an hour and Smith felt that he had convinced them that the cause of the children was a just and urgent one.

But Smith had to wait until 1885 before he could arrange for the Bill he had prepared to be brought before Parliament by his supporters. Known as the 'Movable Dwellings Bill', it included the remedies he had been so assiduously proposing for so long to improve the living condition of the gypsies. Significantly, it did not include the educational clauses; Smith's plans here had already met with some hostility which was to increase later on. The Bill was read a second time but was then blocked, a fate which would become all too familiar with Smith's future Bills. In fact, Smith was bidding fair with his Movable Dwellings Bill to rival the rejection rate of those Bills introduced to reform the anomaly of marriage with a deceased wife's sister. Between 1850 and 1896 there were no fewer than twenty five such Bills introduced into the Commons for this purpose, all of which failed.

Despite the Government's reluctance to get involved in regularising the gypsy mode of life, it offered a sop to Smith by introducing the ninth and tenth clauses of his Bill into their own Housing of the Working Classes Act of 1885. Under this, any "tent, van, shed or similar structure used for human habitation" was brought within the provisions of the Public Health Act of 1875. The sanitary authority was empowered to make by-laws to promote cleanliness in such structures, together with the right to inspect if it felt its regulations were being flouted. Smith wrote upon his copy of the Act: "I have worked hard and long for this (as my books will show), which goes part of the way to improve the poor children's condition." But it was still only part of the way and no further progress could be made during the session.

Meanwhile, the gypsies remained a popular subject for talks, articles and books. Putting darker traits aside for the moment, the attractions of life on the open road (in summer), deep-rooted female interest in palmistry and fortune-telling, plus the usual male speculation about sinuous gypsy beauties all served to keep Smith's reforms before the public. So much so that Smith brought out a popular edition of *I've Been A-Gipsying* in response to encouraging sales.

As a change from writing to the press and addressing Social Science Congresses, he next undertook a lecture tour. He found his audiences in the Young Men's Christian Association and he spoke at Leeds and Hull among other venues. His lectures, of course, were fully reported in the local press and served to keep his crusade alive in the provinces. One of the papers included an interesting description of Smith's physical appearance (he was then fifty-four) and a comment on his platform style. This latter seems seems to have changed over the years, unless the reporter happened to come on a bad night:

> Mr. Smith is a man apparently past middle age, somewhat portly in figure, with a pleasant, kindly face, full and regular features, ornamented with a flowing grey beard turning to white, and surmounted with a good forehead, from which the grey hair is swept backward in curls about his neck. His lecture was read from sheets partly of manuscript and partly of reprint, but he exhibited none of the arts of the elocutionist or the tricks of the actor. In a rough and ready style the sheets were gone through with somewhat of a heroic disregard for the refinements of punctuation.

But the old campaigner still held his audiences, as in former days, with his "moral earnestness, a tone of practical philanthropy and a spirit of genuine human sympathy".

Chapter 15: A Band of Brothers

Smith of Coalville imagines that civilised man
Falls too much in the rear if he lives in a van;
But caravan dwellers, with force and urbanity,
Declare that Smith's views of van life are pure vanity!

Punch

Smith's reputation as a zealous reformer was now well-established in the capital and he was undoubtedly flattered when, in August 1885, he was approached to see if he would be willing to be nominated for the vacant parliamentary seat in the Dulwich division of Camberwell. Smith, much tempted, thought it over carefully and discussed the offer with his wife. Although there was the inherent promise that he would be free to pursue his activities on behalf of the children, especially the travelling children, Smith finally declined, feeling he could do better work outside Parliament.

Early the next year, while he was still battling away drumming up support for a Movable Dwellings Bill, Smith began another venture. This time it was a religious society. Smith was an eccentric character in many ways but this new manifestation of his Christian vision strikes us as more than a little naive. His purpose was to shepherd the poor, the young and the old along the path of righteousness, a path guaranteed to lead them to happiness in this world and to unimaginable bliss in the next. It could be seen as the natural extension of his evangelical endeavours and it was to absorb much of his time and energy until his death. There is little doubt that in moments of harmless vanity he saw himself in the role of the good shepherd; he certainly looked the part.

The genesis of this idea is uncertain. It may well have stemmed from his feeling that thanks to Shaftesbury and other reformers there were no more fields left for him to conquer, no new challenges clamouring to be taken up, no specific class of children suffering abuses that cried out to be rectified. In any case he was growing old; he was past the prime of life and his unceasing exertions had prematurely aged him. He had been disheartened by his lack of success with the Movable Dwellings Bill and the end of the previous year had found him disconsolate and in one of his periodic fits of depression. In a letter to his friend, the Rev. E.A. Hoare, author of *Notable Workers in Humble Life*, he confessed:

> I begin to feel much worse for the wear and tear I have had to pass through in my work. It is a great treat to get a good night's rest... Faith, hope, trust and grace kept me going, step by step.

In February he published a circular from his home in Crick setting out his plans for the establishment of what was to be called, 'The George Smith of Coalville Society and Band of Love'. His Society had three aims:

> i. To unite together in bonds of brotherly love and sympathy persons irrespective of age, sex, sect or party in order to develop the lifework of one George Smith of Coalville. This smacks more than a little of hubris. Yet Smith was wholly sincere in his intentions to lead his brethren, like some latter-day Moses, to the promised land.
>
> ii. To meet, as required, to assist each other 'in love and good works' and to help their poorer brethren achieve positions of respectability in the community.
>
> iii. To collect and distribute among the members and children in need pictures, books of a religious and moral tone, toys, warm clothing and money for education and for other purposes.

To become a brother or sister of the Society one had to complete a standard certificate, sign it and hand it in at a Fellowship meeting to the presiding brother or sister. Then followed an initiation ceremony devised by Smith which he outlined in some detail. After a certain amount of to-ing and fro-ing of hands, it reached a climax with the president kissing the back of the candidate's left hand to symbolize God stooping to receive and welcome the poor. The new brother or sister was then assigned a personal number, a kind of pin-number. At Fellowship meetings he or she greeted other brothers and sisters by shaking hands with the left hand; this apparently was "symbolical of the left hand of society" — whatever that meant. One wonders whether Col. Baden-Powell was aware of this mumbo-jumbo a decade later because the left-handed shake, loyalty to King and country and the duty to help others are salient features of his Scout and Cub organisations.

Thus Smith launched his Christian vision upon an unsuspecting and somewhat cynical public. At first he enjoyed some success, with numerous enquiries from various parts of the country seeking information about how to set up branches of the Society. But only a few were established, such as those at Crick, Walthamstow and Buckby Wharf, where unfortunately the earnest brothers and sisters attracted some hostility and ridicule with their meetings being disrupted.

Smith sent full details of his new Society to Queen Victoria, Princess Beatrice and Sir Henry Ponsonby, requesting that their names be allowed to remain upon the books as first, second and third members respectively, and enclosing their membership certificates. On this occasion he received no reply and he convinced himself that silence meant agreement. This led him shortly afterwards, in a lecture given at Rugby, to declare that "the Queen, Princess Beatrice and Sir Henry Ponsonby were members of the Band of Love". To his dying day, Smith remained convinced that the Queen took an avid interest in all his activities.

At Crick, the branch met in a small building adjoining the Cabin which was later acquired by Grosart, Smith's son, and became known as 'White Cottage'. It is still there today but it has recently been improved out of all recognition. The Fellowship meetings on Sundays were basically Primitive Methodist services with the usual hymns, prayers and lengthy sermon. However, there was a new element introduced into the service by Smith: the Agape or Love-Feast. In the early Christian church the Agape was a meal shared by communicants immediately before the Eucharist. Although the practice fell into disuse, it was revived by John Wesley "that we might together eat bread with gladness and singleness of heart". He also revived the title 'Love-Feast' though "our food is only a little plain cake and water". The idea was embraced whole-heartedly by the Primitive Methodists and Smith in his turn made it central to his meetings.

Apart from their regular Sunday meetings, the Band of Love arranged social events from time to time. Teas and evening entertainments, where there was more on offer than plain cake and water, were highly popular and musical offerings much in demand. The very first tea-meeting of the Crick branch was held at the Founder's house on 11th September, 1886 and was widely reported in the area press. The brothers and sisters paraded through the streets with banners, singing hymns as they went, before breaking up to take part in vigorous games in a nearby field. There followed "an excellent and bountiful tea" for over one hundred perspiring brethren who then listened to a lengthy address by Smith on the subject of George Smith. There were songs by the Misses Smith, Grosart recited 'Gypsy Jim' and Eddie cheered the party up with 'Gelert's Grave'. There were more songs, more

White Cottage and Queen's House

recitations, a solo on the concertina and everyone gave votes of thanks to everyone else. The occasion drew to a close; Smith conducted the National Anthem and as the evening shadows lengthened, the brothers and sisters wandered happily homewards in a blaze of good fellowship.

Although Smith was at one stage sorely tempted to give up the struggle in the face of public apathy towards his Society, he was not, as we know, a man to be easily discouraged once he had set his heart and mind on something. However, four years later, in 1890, there was a most unfortunate incident which virtually finished the Band of Love. In June of that year Smith was subpoenaed to appear at Stratford Police Court against a certain brother called Elias Lamb. Lamb was charged with appropriating sums of money he had collected in the name of George Smith at the Walthamstow branch of the Band of Love. His victim was none other than the well-disposed Duke of Fife who had lost some £13 over six months believing he was sending contributions to Smith via his agent, Lamb. Smith's 'agent' was sentenced to two months hard labour.

This incident confirmed Smith's suspicions about the management of his Society's branches, especially in financial matters. At the time of Lamb's trial Smith had stated that the Society was supported largely by himself. During the four years of its existence the total Smith received from the brothers and sisters in the branches and from contributions from the public did not come to more than £10. It certainly did not cover printing and postage and his travelling expenses which, as usual, he had met out of his own pocket. The Lamb affair certainly took the edge off Smith's enthusiasm for expansion and from this time on he seems to have reduced his involvement apart from continuing to run the two branches of his Society at Crick and nearby Buckby Wharf. He would return from his work and lobbying in London on Saturdays in time to prepare his sermons for the services at Buckby Wharf in the morning and at Crick in the afternoon.

There is no doubt that Smith saw in his new movement a kind of fulfilment he had been denied in his parliamentary struggles. He had been deeply upset at having to give up his Sunday School work in Coalville over ten years earlier and he now exchanged essentially local activity for a somewhat grandiloquent scheme embracing all sorts and conditions of men (and women) nationwide. It was a sincere vision and Smith strove manfully to "reverse the state of things by making the gate to evil narrow, and the gate leading to heaven wide". He struggled on with what was a genuine labour of love but, despite all the determination and energy he poured into it, there were still less than a thousand members all told at the time of his death.

During what proved to be the disheartening and fruitless years 1887–1890, Smith spent ever more time in his cheap lodgings in London. He continued to use the British Museum Reading Room as his office, researching and writing hundreds of letters. Much of his time was spent haunting the Houses of Parliament, especially in the evenings. Night after night he was to be found in the Commons lobby pressing his case upon unwary members. His sincerity was undoubted but his relentless campaigning for the gypsy children, the narrowness of his vision and his refusal to come to terms with practical politics were losing him support.

Smith worked doggedly on, seeking support for what was becoming an increasingly unpopular measure. He would sit in the Strangers Gallery till midnight, lingering, to quote Hodder, "in the fond belief that his presence there was facilitating the progress of the Bill". All this was of no avail. Session after session H.C. Stephens, the MP for Hornsey, he of the ink, would announce "I object"; in one year he and Tomlinson, the member for Preston, blocked the Bill more than sixty times.

When he was not lurking in the Lobby or following the progress of his various Bills in the Chamber, or working in the Reading Room, he spent most of his spare time visiting gypsy sites in and around London. He was intent on gathering yet more material with which to bombard and convince ministers of the urgent need for legislation, particularly over the vexed question of education. In this connection he records a typical encounter with a ragged and dirty gypsy lad in Epping Forest:

> I asked what his name was. He answered, 'I don't know; I've got so many names. Sometimes they call me Smith, sometimes Brown, and lots of other names' — 'Have you ever been washed in your life?' — 'Not that I know of, sir.' — 'Were you ever in a school?' — 'No' — 'Did you ever hear of Jesus?' — 'I never heard of such a man; He does not live up in this forest'. — 'Where does God live?' — 'I don't know. I never heard of him neither. There used to be a chap lived in the Forest with a name like that, but he's been gone away a long time. I think he went a-hoppin' in Kent'.

Smith felt that the Housing of the Working Classes Act of 1885 was still inadequate for his purposes and had done little more than prepare the way for future legislation. So in 1887 he prepared a measure known as the Temporary Dwellings Bill and, with most of the press supporting him, arranged with the help of Burt and other sympathetic MPs for it to be introduced. This time it included the educational clauses. The Bill was read a second time and then referred to a Select Committee. All through the summer, night after night, Smith attended the House watching over the progress of his Bill. Yet all turned to dust; at the end of the session the Government abandoned the Bill on the grounds of cost and shelved it for another year. It was not simply a matter of money; there were strong objections to the education proposals. Smith made much of the similarity between boat children and gypsy children, his 'little nomads', but it was much harder to deal with those living in mobile tents and vans than with those living in similar squalor in slow-moving narrow boats on the canals. Punch suggested the solution might be the use of "a flying column of elementary school teachers, who, mounted say on bicycles, might pursue the illiterate enemy through the roads and lanes, and engage him in pitched battles on the pleasant commons, where he may generally be found in force".

The teachers, too, were hostile to the Bill. They protested that the arrival of the gypsy children in their schools would bring their own pupils under the contaminating influence of those whom George Smith himself had shown to be exposed to gross indecency and moral laxity. There was, of course, an element of self-interest underlying their attitude. At this time teachers were operating under the Revised Code of 1862, a system commonly called payment by results. Grants for staff salaries could only be earned on pupils under twelve and depended on their making a certain number of attendances; they were also subject to the results of an examination by the Government Inspector of each child in reading, writing and arithmetic. Fewer examination successes meant less money for the staff; attempting to inculcate the three R's into children who could only attend irregularly would seriously affect their salaries. The Revised Code was watered down in minor ways by successive administrations until it was finally abandoned in 1897.

In 1888 the Temporary Dwellings Bill was brought in yet again by Thomas Burt but this time under a lengthy new title, 'A Bill to provide for the Registration and Regulation of Travelling Vans and other Vehicles used as Temporary Abodes'. At Smith's insistence it still included the educational clauses. The change of title did it little good, however, for it was considered a 'drastic measure' and again blocked. Stephens, was to prove an implacable opponent and a thorn in the flesh for Smith over the next few years. Refusing to accept defeat, Smith drew up a shorter Bill entitled the Movable Abodes Bill. This was read a second time, after a struggle, but to his chagrin was then promptly shelved for the session.

At least the year ended on a somewhat happier note. On the 16th November Smith received an unusual and unexpected present which gave him great pleasure. The Lee family, one of the oldest and foremost families in the Romani community, presented him with a rather special small copper and brass box bearing the name of Right Door Lee, engraved and dated one thousand one hundred and ninety seven (1197). This dubious heirloom, for which Smith paid David Lee one pound, was "a token of goodwill for his long efforts to improve our condition and educate our children". Lee said it was "handed to me by my father, Zachariah Lee, over thirty years ago, and which was held from his father and ancestors back to the date shown on the mystical box". The Lees made one stipulation; the box should never go out of Smith's family but should be preserved as a curiosity and as a token of their goodwill. Today the box (which I have seen) is still in the possession of Smith's descendants.

Early in 1889 Smith took steps to have his 'Temporary Dwellings Bill' re-introduced into Parliament. It was read a second time with the help of the Government on the understanding that more administrative power should be given to the new County Councils established in the previous year. Smith swiftly produced a new and shorter Bill for this purpose — the Movable

Dwellings Bill — but he was stymied yet again by Stephens. Stephens claimed that the effect of the Bill would be to drive the travellers "from their harmless and healthy country life into our overcrowded towns". He shared the strong sentimental feeling among the public that the gypsies were entitled to their traditional nomadic way of life and that, despite the difficulties their habits created, they should be allowed to pursue it unhindered by bureaucrats inside Parliament and council officers outside.

In addition to initial objections to the educational clauses and to a concern that the gypsies' traditional freedom of movement might be jeopardised, there arose what was to prove the main stumbling block. What stuck in the craw of some people and led to increasing opposition to the Bill was the clause authorising any officer of a county or sanitary authority (thus including the police) to enter and examine a gypsy's or hawker's van at any time between six in the morning and nine at night, or, if he had armed himself with a magistrate's warrant, at any time during the rest of the night. This proposal went far beyond what had been accepted as appropriate for the inspection of canal boats. It was construed by opponents of the Bill as a violation of the sacred rights of property, and the principle that an Englishman's house is his castle, even if it was no better than a ragged tent or an old van, was invoked.

Stephens was also an active member of the Liberty and Property Defence League which now appears on the scene and he voiced their criticisms. He considered the sanitary aim of the Bill was amply provided for under the Housing of the Working Classes Act of 1885; that the educational powers were useless and, if introduced, would damage the elementary schools. He declared: "If any attempts are made to enforce it, very vehement and unsurmountable opposition on the part of school managers and school teachers will certainly be exacted". He added for good measure that the registration of movable dwellings, even if it were possible to define them, was unnecessary, and that the power of entry at night was without parallel and fraught with problems. In brief, he condemned the Bill out of hand as "uncalled for, injurious, cruelly oppressive, and very ill-considered as an administrative proposal".

Stephen's objections in the House were echoed outside Parliament by Lord Wemyss, one of the leaders of the League. Wemyss objected strenuously to the power of entry into any gypsy dwelling at any time on a magistrates order after nine p.m. "What!" he exclaimed, "Is this not a gross violation of the rights of the subject? Every gypsy's van is his castle, and he should be at liberty to make a pig-sty of it if he likes." Smith, of course, also believed strongly in the liberty of the subject but not when that liberty meant bringing up children in ignorance and vice.

Because this controversy aroused a great deal of comment in the press an attempt was made to achieve some sort of compromise between the interested parties. A meeting was arranged involving Smith, Stephens and two other MPs, Long and Sir W. Hart-Dyke. Smith had already offered to accept any amendment put forward by Stephens as long as it did not undermine the main proposals of his Bill. But Stephens made no effort to meet him and put forward no suggestions whatsoever. He refused to budge an inch and the meeting broke up with a solution as far away as ever.

It is hardly surprising that the cumulative effects of his exertions, travels, frustration and disappointments began to undermine even Smith's formidable constitution. The constant obstructionist tactics of Stephens and his cronies disheartened him and he suffered fits of depression. A newspaper described the nightly ritual Smith endured in the House:

> .... from the opposite benches comes the fatal, 'I object', and then the aged philanthropist gets up from his seat, and with bent head and saddened face goes out into the lobby and home. Thus the persistent and relentless opposition of a single member is able to frustrate, year after year, the efforts of a good man to improve the lot of perhaps the most helpless and most wretched of his fellow creatures.

Smith was now over sixty and he wondered if he would ever see his Bill on the statute book. He wrote in his diary in July:

> To all appearance the Movable Dwellings Bill I have had in hand for so many long years will not become law this session — perhaps never! By the obstruction of three or four members who have persistently blocked this measure, fifty thousand children have been kept in ignorance and amid scenes of vice. This Bill will kill me if God does not interpose.

Still feeling unwell, he became concerned about his heart. His doctor told him there was nothing wrong with his heart but that he had a "bad gastric catarrh on the stomach", was overworked and needed rest. It is not clear what the doctor meant (we have only Smith's version from his diary) but this may have been the first indication of the presence of the disease which would eventually kill him. Typically, Smith ignored his doctor's advice and continued as before, but he admitted a few days later, "I feel sick and languid at times, and almost wish to see the end of my journey".

Meanwhile, the secretary of the League, alert to the implications of the Bill for travellers other than the gypsies, had stirred up a hornet's nest by getting in touch with the all the leading showmen. He pointed out that it was now not merely the gypsies who were being threatened with legislation but the showmen and fairground operators as well. The League appealed "to every owner and occupier of a travelling-van, cart, wagon, vehicle or tent which is used as a dwelling or sleeping place" to rise up in protest and defeat the iniquitous Movable Dwellings Bill.

The showmen were soon up in arms and they proved an organised and articulate minority. On 28 January 1891 they met at the Agricultural Hall in London and formed the United Kingdom Showmen and Van Dwellers Association (UKSVDA) "to protest against George Smith, his libellous statements, and his detestable Bill". The Association's immediate aim was to defeat the Bill but it also proposed to vet legislation directed against van-dwellers, to assist members with legal aid and to set up a distress fund. It had neither the power nor the intention of regulating the day-to-day running of the fairs. Lord George Sanger was the driving force behind the Association but all the famous showmen of the time were involved in these early proceedings, Pat Collins, Bostock of Bostock & Wombwell's Menageries, the Studts of Wales, McIndoes of Scotland, and Murphys from the North-East.

This was the first time the showmen had banded together to resist external legislation. Fairs had been the object of interference and legislation, locally and nationally, for three hundred years, and during this period the showmen had been discriminated against by the authorities. But now they were no longer the quasi-vagabonds of the early part of the century. The ride-owners had a considerable investment to protect. Sanger's circus had been shown to the Queen; Bostock's menagerie travelled on the Continent, while Pat Collins owned thirty traction engines. They saw themselves as respectable members of the business community with money in the bank, employees and a good name to protect. They were in no mood to succumb to external threats.

Stephens was in the chair at the meeting and when he demanded action he was cheered to the echo. Smith, quite unconcerned for his safety, also attended and had to listen to one of the showmen declare to great applause:

> My father and grandfather before me were travellers. I was born in a van, and I hope to God I shall die in a van.... Now, sir, you spoke about accidents happening when men in private clothes come snooping about.

I'll tell you this, sir, that if a man comes peeping into my Caravan when my wife and children are abed, I'll make good use of the means God has given man for defending himself.

When at last Smith spoke, his speech was greeted with boos and jeers, especially when he claimed a divine right to elevate his little nomads and refused point-blank to admit the claims of the UKSVDA. He aroused such animosity that he had to be hustled out the back way.

The rowdy meeting was fully reported in the press the next day and it became obvious that the tide of public sympathy for Smith and his endeavours was on the ebb. Smith was now faced with an unholy alliance between the League championing the gypsies' cause, with its supporters in the House strenuously opposing aspects of his Bill, and the new UKSVDA flexing its muscles on behalf of the fairground operators. This boded ill for Smith; it never occurred to him that he might have taken a rather one-sided view of the situation, or might have fallen into that trap for unwary and unworldly reformers — exaggerating the evils he was fighting against. The effect of this meeting was unmistakable; Smith had lost ground he was never to regain.

In 1892 the UKSVDA felt strong enough to hold its first AGM at the Agricultural Hall. The showmen decided to keep up the pressure on Smith and they organised a series of protest meetings throughout the country, some of which Smith attended. One can only admire yet again Smith's courage in taking on the showmen almost single-handed and putting his head, as it were, into the lion's mouth so often. He was quite aware of the reception that awaited him at these venues and he confessed to being more than a little apprehensive. But when the time came he spoke up boldly on behalf of the van children, enduring the storms of abuse hurled at him and carrying on unmoved.

The results were predictable; at Peterborough Great Fair he was jostled and man-handled, while at York the showmen swore they would never allow him to make an appeal through the press without taking action themselves. A meeting at the Rotherham Statutes Fair passed a resolution protesting against the Bill "promoted by Mr. George Smith of Crick, Rugby, as being subversive to the liberties of Englishmen and injurious to the best interests of showmen and others who gain their livelihood travelling from fair to fair." At Birmingham Fair a leading showman told him that if he went to their meeting he had orders from headquarters to bring up his men and drum him out. Smith, never one to shirk a challenge, made a point of going to the meeting. He clambered onto the platform and faced the hostile audience. When the shouting had died down, he recalled:

> I told them, with their clenched fists and white teeth facing me, that I was not the man, and never was and never shall be, to be frightened by drums and threats out of my life's work, until I have carried the flag of the gypsy and van children to victory, as I did for the brick-yard and canal children.

Stout-hearted as he was, victory was to be denied him. A few months later, reviewing his labours on behalf of the gypsy children, Smith was forced to admit: "I have not directly succeeded in passing beyond the Committee stages any of my own Bills during the last ten years." His only consolation was that, as a result of his agitation and pressure upon the Government, he could point to two recent minor successes. First, missionary agencies and temperance societies had been started by friends living in many of the large towns and cities in England and Scotland where gypsies tended to gather. Secondly, the Medical Officer of Health for Nottingham in his annual report for 1890 had commented, in referring to 'Dwelling Vans', that:

> The condition of these structures as a class had greatly improved during recent years. This is probably in a great measure owing to the increased attention they have received from the public through the agency of one philanthropic agitator, who has espoused the cause of the van dwellers.

Chapter 16: Journey's End

> The unity, consistency, and perseverance of his life were wonderful. He took human suffering and human sorrow, and the helplessness of childhood, and the poor, as an end for which to live.
>
> Cardinal Manning after reading
> Hodder's *Life of Lord Shaftesbury*

The year 1893 brought little relief and less encouragement for our philanthropic agitator. No sooner had he celebrated Christmas and New Year with his family at Crick than he was down in London in early January to attend the second AGM of the UKSVDA. This turned out to be something of a bizarre affair. It happened to coincide with the six weeks stay of the World Fair and nearly six hundred members turned up for the meeting, many of them in circus rig, "rouged and wigged and dressed in fantastic costumes". Smith attended with a small group of friends, sitting composed and smiling amid a shower of taunts and jeers for several hours. Even Lord George Sanger was forced to admire his sang-froid, stating later that "to have smiled through all those hours of vituperative challenge was a histrionic feat of which Henry Irving might feel proud".

Because of the continuing hostility towards his Movable Dwellings Bill, Smith, reluctantly, had been forced to modify it. He removed any suggestion that the police might be involved in inspecting dwellings and he agreed that the sanitary laws were not to apply to children under twelve. At the end of March the revised Bill was again brought forward. Smith travelled down to London and haunted the lobby at Westminster, seeking support from former friends and acquaintances. By this time, however, these had become more than a little weary of his persistence and had rather lost patience with him. Smith's lobbying was to no purpose. Stephens continued his block on the Bill and he was supported more vociferously than ever by the Liberty and Property Defence League and the UKSVDA. Both organisations realised they were winning the argument and so they kept the pressure up during the early summer with another series of protest meetings in the Midlands and the North.

Meanwhile, Smith continued to visit gypsy camps and gatherings explaining to those who would listen the benefits of his Bill and trying to reassure them about nocturnal inspections by officials. On many of these visits he found that the League and the showmen had been before him spreading false rumours about his intentions and sensed a distinct coolness in his reception. For example, at Ascot in mid-June he met some gypsies who told him that leaflets were being circulated among the gypsies and travellers stressing that Smith meant to take away from their parents all those gypsy and van children under fourteen years of age. This suggestion of the forcible removal of children to attend school triggered the Romani's traditional fear that emancipation of a child through education might lead to their leaving the family for good. Smith replied that this was a pack of lies, whereupon:

> One black gipsy woman, a Cooper, came at me like a lioness with fire in her eyes, fire in her fists, and fire in her tongue, which brought up another black Cooper, a man who threatened my life. Some Lees and others came to my help, and after a time, with tact and self-control, I retired from the field with scores of gypsy and van children round me as a bodyguard to the high road.... I next went to the race course to face angry looks and threatening language. The Coopers said that if I went upon the course I should not come off alive. Two rough chaps bawled out, 'Burn him alive!' and a woman said she would like to empty a barrel of paraffin over me and set fire to it!

The UKSVDA had done their work well. An example of how far they were prepared to go to discredit Smith occurred in the autumn. A group of showmen organised a meeting at Coalville late one afternoon in October with a carefully selected audience. Smith had paid several visits to Coalville since he had left for Welton in 1880. The last occasion was at Whitsun in 1891 when he was pleased to find he was generally welcomed by the miners and other working people who had come to appreciate his efforts over the years on behalf of their children. But there were still what he called "circles of little souls and haters" who could neither forget nor forgive. The meeting was poorly attended and the handful of Smith's friends and supporters who attempted to put his case were shouted down and their efforts went unreported. A resolution having little relevance to the purpose of the meeting was passed, indicating that the ill-feeling of a section of the townspeople towards Smith had not diminished with the years:

> "That this meeting of the inhabitants of Coalville indignantly protests against the continued and unwarrantable assumption of their town's good

name, by a person styling himself "George Smith of Coalville', who is neither a native nor a resident of the town!" They have long memories in Coalville and brood upon imagined wrongs!

In the late autumn Smith's hopes revived briefly. The Parish Councils Bill was under discussion in Parliament and Smith made strenuous efforts to get the Government to take powers under it to bring the dwellings of gypsy and other travelling children under simple, uniform, sanitary regulations. He argued that the Parish Councils would have authority over dogs, drains, roads, houses and village greens but they would have no control over those living in movable dwellings on village greens. He lobbied hard for a clause to be inserted vesting such power in the Parish Councils. The Government demurred; the Bill, it said, was too heavily weighted already to extend its provisions in this way. But Smith did achieve one small reform. A short clause was eventually inserted giving councils some control over tents and vans that camped on the village greens and other open spaces. Smith hoped that this would make the van-dwellers realise it would be in their interest to ensure vans were in an acceptable state and to see their children brought under the Education Code. And with this he had to be content.

Smith had given up active party politics many years ago, though he remained an ardent Radical at heart. Then quite unexpectedly his interest was re-kindled. He was approached to become the Chairman of the Crick Liberal Association. As we have seen, his main local interest during his time in Crick had been the Band of Love, but Smith was happy to accept what was hardly an onerous office. The local Liberals were delighted to recruit such a well-known and formidable figure as their chairman. Smith took his role seriously. At the Parish and District Council elections in December, which were run on party lines, he became a candidate. Although a mixed Parish Council was returned, Smith received little support and failed to get elected. His flame was thus unkindly doused.

During the early part of 1894 the feeling steadily grew, even among his friends and supporters, that his proposed Bill was far too harsh, and that, if passed, would have the effect of "improving the van-dweller off the face of the earth". The policy of the various groups opposing his measure was now the rather subtle one of favouring parts of the Bill while strongly opposing others and thus weakening it as a whole. The truth was that the UKSVDA continued to gain ground; as it did so, Smith's hopes and health started to wane.

George Smith aged 63

He visibly began to tire and to weaken. There were still flashes of the old pugnacity and determination but the stamina and resilience which had carried him through his arduous campaigns in all weathers and against all comers had declined. Although by modern standards he was still only in late middle age, his body could no longer respond to the demands of his courageous spirit. Smith became concerned about his health and in the autumn he was advised to consult a Dr. Guttendigg of Harley Street but the specialist was unable to offer a diagnosis.

As he found it increasingly difficult to get about, he went to Banbury one day at the end of November to look at a pony and trap belonging to a gypsy namesake, George Smith, "to help the infirmities of my poor body". The horse was old and slow but the trap and harness were in good condition and

Smith paid £10 for the outfit. Even this minor excursion was almost too much for him, as he wrote in his diary the following day: "November 30, 1894: I seemed to be at the door of death, and staggered out for a nip of brandy or whisky to keep me from fainting". An admission this from a lifelong total abstainer!

The spasms of pain he had suffered in the last months were increasing in duration and severity, and he was now in considerable discomfort, as he records: "December 17: Ill all day. My life is ebbing out into the ocean of eternity.

December 18: Nearer to the gates of death. Twice in my room I thought I should have died."

With typical determination he travelled down to London on 27th December to attend a special meeting arranged by friends at Sion College on the Embankment. This Gothic style building, established for the benefit of Anglican clergy, was a recent adornment to the north bank of the Thames. Situated halfway between Temple Gardens and Cubitt's Blackfriars Bridge, it was built in 1886 to the design of Sir Arthur Blomfield and incorporated the original timber roof from its former home on London Wall. In these splendid surroundings Smith was presented with his portrait painted by C.H. Blair and a purse of two hundred and twenty-five pounds collected from his many friends. The actual presentation was made by an old friend and ally, the editor, W.T. Stead. It was Stead who, years before when he was editor of the *Pall Mall Gazette*, had helped Smith in his work by organising a subscription for his benefit. Smith, weak and ill, was close to tears and found it difficult to reply to this manifestation of kindness and esteem. Such a day, he declared, helped him to forget past difficulties and disappointments and he told his friends that he intended to strive to "complete the work that lies so close to my heart".

The New Year ushered in a period of severe weather. Heavy snowfalls blanketed the Midlands and the canals were frozen up. Smith had felt for some time that the walk every Sunday to Long Buckby Wharf to take the service for the Band of Love was becoming too much for him and now the gypsy's pony and trap came into its own in earnest. But it was still a tiring journey and at the end of it he rarely found more than fifteen people present. Smith gritted his teeth and persisted, as he continued to do with his Movable Dwellings Bill.

He went to London in a snowstorm in early February when the Bill was once more before the House to lobby sympathetic MPs. This was the last time he would do so. He stayed on in London for a while, grateful for the warmth of the Reading Room. He still visited editors and journalists to press his case, always returning to the House of Commons in the evenings to monitor the progress, if any, of his Bill. Eventually he would make his way late at night, "cold, sick and weary", to his lodgings, there "to suffer much with cramp and cold". But it was all to no avail. His Bill was again rejected and Smith finally seems to have recognised that no further progress was possible. Despite all the labour and humiliations of the last fifteen years, he realised his ambition would now never be achieved. It left him saddened and exhausted.

Towards the end of February the pain became worse and the entries in his diary became less frequent. The last entry in a diary he had kept meticulously for eighteen years read: "March 6. Ill. I feel cast down. My life's work is closing. O Lord my God, in thee do I put my trust".

It gave him much pleasure to paste into his great black book a cutting from the *Lancet* giving an account of the 23rd Annual Report of the Local Government Board. This cheered him immensely for it contained an account by John Brydone about the condition of the canal boats:

> In concluding his report, Mr. Brydone affirms emphatically that the Acts continue to exert the most beneficial influence upon the boat population, and that they have operated in a high degree in reducing the number of women and children travelling in the boats. The women are, he reports, feeling more and more that the canal-boat employment is not a fitting one for them, and that cabin homes are not proper places for the rearing of young children.

Smith marked the passage in the margin and wrote against it, "Thank God!".

A few days after Easter he visited his doctor who advised him to spend a month at the seaside. So he and Mary travelled down to Ramsgate in the hope that sea air and new surroundings would help him to recover his spirits. Despite feeling wretched, Smith lost no time in contacting the editor of the *Thanet Advertiser*, and gave him a detailed account of his life and campaigns. He complained about the opposition to his latest Bill in and outside Parliament and discussed the possible effects the recent Parish Councils Act might have on its progress. All this was duly printed. Sadly, the pain became more insistent, and on his return to The Cabin Smith arranged an appointment with another doctor in Rugby who correctly diagnosed cancer of the liver. Smith took the news stoically. He was forced to take to his bed early in June; Mary nursed him devotedly while his daughters, Clara and Beatrice, looked after the house. They even had a harmonium brought up to his bedroom so that he could join them in the hymns he particularly loved.

It was now time for taking stock of his life and for preparing to meet his God. Smith had said on several occasions that he was not afraid of death and his unwavering faith lent him a dignity and a serenity remarked on by all who saw him. He looked back on the switchback nature of his business career and his struggles on behalf of the children with a certain satisfaction. To his wife and daughters, who had borne years of hardship without complaint, he confided, "I have been a misunderstood man all my life". He received a constant stream of visitors anxious to pay their last respects to a doughty old fighter who was sinking fast. One of his regular visitors was his great friend, J.L. Paton a master at Rugby School. Smith was all too aware of his limitations and he confessed to Paton as he lay dying, "I never was a joker; perhaps it would have been better for me if I had been, but I always took life in a serious way".

The end was not far off. He was now unable to manage any solids and for a fortnight he took nothing but ice. On the Sunday before he died the Primitive Methodist Brass Band of Rugby held a service under his open window. This would not be everyone's taste on their death-bed and with only a little time left for quiet contemplation, but Smith apparently enjoyed it. On 20th June Smith, sensing the approach of the 'Old Chap', asked his wife and children to gather round his bed, It was to be another Victorian death-bed scene, rather like that of his father years before. First, they sang one of his favourite hymns, "For ever with the Lord". Then Smith roused himself and gave clear instructions regarding his funeral, his grave and certain family matters. He expressed a wish to be buried in one particular spot in the churchyard at Crick —the open place near the school where he could hear the children sing. "If they are not near to my bed when I die, they will be near to my heart". He next gave each of his children a Bible in which he had written, accurately but perhaps rather dramatically, "A present from my dying bed". Finally, he spoke to his eldest son: "Grosart, a heavy responsibility rests on you; but cast thy burden on the Lord and He will sustain thee". A little later he slipped into a coma and in twenty four hours he was dead.

His coffin was moved downstairs and placed in the Band of Love room adjoining The Cabin. The brass plate on the coffin bore the inscription "George Smith of Coalville, the children's friend, born Feb. 1831, died June 21st. 1895." The next morning there was a short service held in the room taken by his old friend the Rev. W. J. Woods, who had first known Smith when he was a manager at Coalville. It was attended by his widow, the sons and daughters of both his marriages and a number of close friends. Then the coffin was carried out to the hearse and the cortege made its way to the Parish Church of St. Margaret, the chief mourners riding in carriages and friends following in procession behind. The rear was brought up by fifty members of the Band of Love carrying small posies. There was a brief service in the crowded Parish Church and after the coffin had been lowered into the grave there was a hymn and a further address by the Rev. R. Spears, editor of *Christian Life*, followed by prayers. One after another the members of the Band of Love filed past the grave and dropped their posies onto the coffin. The mourners slowly began to drift away. It had been one of the most impressive funerals ever seen at Crick.

Mary Smith and her family lingered by the graveside in the sunshine for a little while and then made their way slowly to the church gate and the waiting carriages.

The church lies close to the crossroads of this quiet unassuming village. Smith's grave is not difficult to find. Entering by the church gate, bear right along the path for some forty yards and the grave, marked by a stone cross, lies a few yards away on your right. The lettering on the cross needs cleaning but the inscription reads as follows:

> *George Smith of Coalville*
> *Who died at Crick*
> *June 21 1895*
> *Aged 65 years**

followed by the somewhat lack-lustre and confusing comment:

> *To Thee it was Given Many*
> *To Save With Thyself and*
> *At the End of the Day*
> *O Faithful Shepherd to Come*
> *Bringing Thy Sheep in Thy Hand*

---

* This is incorrect; he was 64.

On the base of the cross is a brief tribute to his wife, Mary, who continued to live in Crick for another twenty years:

> *Also Mary Ann*
> *The Beloved Wife of the Above*
> *Who Died at Crick*
> *May 1917 Aged 83 Years*
>
> *A Faithful helpmate*

Such was the passing of 'The Children's Friend'. Smith went to his grave with his final reform still unachieved. Further attempts to pass a Movable Dwellings Bill the following year proved unsuccessful. It was not until the resurgence of the Gypsy Lore Society in the early years of the twentieth century that the success which had eluded Smith for so many years finally came to pass. The Society was revived through the efforts of some fresh enthusiasts notably John Sampson (compiler of the first Romani dictionary and close friend of Augustus John), Scott Macfie and David MacRitchie, who re-launched the Journal in 1907. As a result, new impetus was given to reform and by 1936 all Smith's cherished objectives, except registration, were incorporated in various Acts of Parliament. So one might claim a posthumous victory for him.

After his death a few dissenting voices were heard among the general plaudits. Several contended that Smith had sacrificed his second wife and children for the sake of his career, though this charge hardly stands up to examination. Despite the poverty and hardships of his middle years, he managed to secure a sound education for his children and see them launched on successful careers. Of his two surviving sons by his first marriage, George became an architect and Charles a schoolmaster. Of his children by his second wife, Grosart became a doctor, Eddy emigrated to a new life in South Africa and Smith arranged for his two daughters, Clara and Beatrice, to attend the Unitarian school in Highgate. It seems unlikely that he found all the money for their fees and expenses out of his own pocket. The various sums of money he received at long intervals were swallowed up in meeting his immediate needs and settling his debts. This suggests the intervention of good friends, whose generosity he was always quick to acknowledge.

Resentment also lingered, especially in the Coalville area, at his perseverance in unpopular causes, his obstinacy, and his outspokenness. Throughout his life Smith believed he had a divine call and that all his actions and activities, even the most mundane such as travelling and letter-writing, were ordered and guided by God. This made him a man difficult to overcome in argument and one unlikely to change his mind or alter his chosen course of action. Smith cheerfully acknowledged his weaknesses, made little attempt to remedy them, and refused to compromise on what he saw as his divine mission.

The death of a man who could be described with some justice as the poor man's Shaftesbury was widely mourned. He was particularly missed by the boatmen and their families and by most Romani, who realised they had lost an old and valued friend. The public, too, sensed the passing of a humble champion of the poor, one who, without a thought of personal reward or advancement, had waged a lonely struggle all his life against ignorance, prejudice and the exploitation of children. His death went unnoticed by the national press but obituaries in the papers serving the Midlands were deservedly fulsome. It is fitting for this book to end with a passage from the one in the local paper of his home town, the *Potteries Examiner*. It illustrates the esteem in which Smith finally came to be held by the Victorian public:

> He has been a benefactor to children, and his name and memory in connection with his tireless exertions, self-denying zeal, and generous and unpaid labours, will be fragrant and pleasant when beneath the green sod he sleeps the sleep of the just.

Books by George Smith

The Cry of the Children from the Brickyards of England, with Remedy. London: Simpkin, Marshall & Co. 1871.

Our Canal Population. A Cry from the Boat Cabins. With Remedy. London: Haughton & Co. 1875. New Edition, with Supplement. London: same imprint. 1879.

And How the Cry has been heard. With Observations upon the carrying out of the Act. Sixth Edition. London: Haughton & Co. 1879.

Gypsy Life: being an (Historical) Account of our Gypsies and their Children. With suggestions for their improvement London: Haughton and Co. 1880.

Canal Adventures by Moonlight. London: Hodder and Stoughton. 1881.

I've been A Gypsying. A Ramble among our Gypsies and other Children in their Tents and Vans. London: Fisher Unwin.' 1884. Popular Edition, 1885.

Our Canal, Gypsy, Van, and other Travelling Children. Privately printed. 1885.

Gypsy Children. A Stroll in Gypsydom, with Songs and Stories. London: Printed and published by Woodford, Fawcett and Co. 1889.

An Open Letter; or Sorrows and Joys of Bosvil. Leek: M.H. Miller. 1892.

Select Bibliography

George Smith (of Coalville): The Story of an Enthusiast, Edwin Hodder. James Nesbitt & Co. Ltd., London, 1896.

Methodism, Rupert Davies. Penguin Books, 1963.

A History of Factory Legislation, B.L. Hutchins and A. Harrison. P.S. King & Son Ltd., London, 1926.

Bricks and Brickmaking, Martin Hammond. Shire Publications Ltd.

Brick-yard Children: an answer to the charges of Mr. George Smith against The Tileries, Tunstall John N. Peake Grant & Co., London, 1871.

The Canal Boatmen 1760–1914, Harry Hanson. Manchester University Press, 1975.

'Social Policy and the Floating Population', Raymond Macleod. Article in *Past and Present,* 1966.

Rob Rat: A Story of Barge Life, Mark Guy. Pearse T. Woolmar, London, 1885.

Gypsies of Britain: an introduction to their history, Vesey-Fitzgerald B. David and Charles, 1973.

The Gypsies, Angus Fraser. Blackwell, 1992.

Notable Workers in Humble Life, Rev. E.A. Hoare MA. Thomas Nelson and Sons, 1887.

Coalville: the first 75 years, Denis Baker. Leicestershire Museum Service, 1983.

Index

Acrobats 137, 138, 142
Alton Grange 38
An Open Letter to my Friends 7, 39, 91
Association for the Promotion of
    Social Science 59, 114
Baird, Rev.John 148
Baker, Robert 44, 45, 47, 48, 53, 66–8, 70, 72, 73, 75, 82, 107, 117
Band of Love 155-8, 168, 170, 172, 173
Blair, C.H. 170
Boatmen's Mission 104
Borrow, George 141
Bourne, Hugh 30
Brick-making 21-6, 46
Brick-yard children Chs 5 & 6
Brick-yard Masters Association 61, 73
Broadhurst, Henry, MP 120, 125
Brontë, Charlotte 81
Browning, Elizabeth Barrett 65, 66
Browning, Robert 59
Bruce, H.A. (Lord Aberdare) 59, 65, 70, 73-6, 114, 124
Brydone, John 125, 127, 171
Burritt, Elihu 24, 69
Burt, Thomas, M.P. 151, 160

Cabin, The 7, 128, 129, 171
Canal Adventures by Moonlight 112, 118, 120, 122, 147
Canal Association 109
Canal Boats Act 1877 109, 110, 112, 113, 124, 131
Canal Boats Act 1877, Amendment
    Bill, 1884 121, 123, 124, 126, 131, 146, 151
Canal Hall 12
Canal children 99, 100, 105, 122, 126
Canals 15, 16, 94–6, 103, 110, 118
Church Congress 106, 107
Circuses 136, 137, 139, 166
Clayhills 14–8, 31, 34, 52, 87, 94
Clowes, William 30
Coalville 35–7, 39, 42, 51, 64, 65, 76, 79, 80, 88, 91, 119, 167, 173, 174

Coalville House 37, 39, 120
Corbet, John, MP 113
Crick 128, 129, 156, 158, 166, 168, 172, 173
Cross, Sir Richard 108, 109, 152
Cry, The Cry of the Children 12, 17, 28, 51, 65, 66, 68, 69, 72, 105

Dame Schools 17–9, 67
Dial House 90, 91
Dickens, Charles 26, 63, 137, 139, 140
Dilke, Sir Charles 123, 151, 152
Disraeli, Benjamin 81-4, 114, 117
Drood, Edwin 63

Education Act, 1870 58, 113
Education Act 1876 108
Factories Acts (Brick and Tile Yards)
    Extension Bill 1871 68, 70, 74, 77, 79, 85, 102
Factories and Workshop Act
    (Consolidation) 1878 49
Factory Act 1833 45, 47, 69
Factory Act 1844 56, 69
Factory Act 1864 48, 49, 69, 72, 73, 77
Factory and Workshops
    Act Commission 49, 107
Factory Acts Extension Act 1867 48, 49, 69, 70
Fairground operators 136, 163, 164
Forster, W.E., MP 58, 113, 114, 124

Gaskell, Peter, *Artisans and Machinery* 27
Gladstone, William 60, 61, 67, 81, 83, 84, 117, 120, 121
Grosart, Rev. A.B. 11, 75
Gypsies 95, Chs 13 & 14, 167
Gypsy Lore Society 142, 174
Gypsy Life 143, 144, 149

Half-time system 56
Hanani or Memoir of William Smith 11, 42
Hanson, Harry 8

Harcourt, Sir William, MP	121	Oastler, Richard	9, 47
Hard Times	137	*Old Curiosity Shop, The*	139–41
Hardy, Thomas	29, 65	*Our Canal Population*	105, 106, 122
Hill, Stavely, QC MP	109	*Ouse*	118, 119
Hoare, Rev. E.A.	155		
Hodder, Edwin	7, 8, 80, 125, 128, 143, 158	Paget, Thomas Tertius	75, 81–4
		Peake, John Nash	62–4, 71–4, 77, 78
Hollins, Hannah	13–6	Peake's Tileries	15, 16, 19, 20, 23, 24, 31, 59, 62, 63, 74, 130
Housing of the Working Classes Act, 1885	152, 159, 160	Pearce, Rev. Guy (*Rob Rat*)	122
Humberstone	34, 35, 36, 38	Plimsoll, Samuel	9, 11
		Potteries	11, 14, 15, 19, 33, 59, 77, 87
I've been A Gypsying	149, 150, 153		
		Queen's Cottage	34
Kirk Yetholme	148	Queen's House	7, 129
Ladderedge	31–3	Raikes, Robert	17
Lamb, Elias	157, 158	Reapsmoor	32, 34, 38
Leek	31, 32	Redgrave, Alexander	56, 70
Legging	118	Reform Bill 1832	81
Lehman, Mary Ann	51	Retorm Bill 1867	82
Leicester	39, 81, 82, 84, 89, 91, 107	Reports of Inspectors of Factories	45, 46
Leicestershire	80–2, 84	Royal Bounty Fund	127, 128
Liberty and Property Defence League	161, 163, 167	Sadler, Michael	9, 47
Local Government Board	108–10, 113, 116, 120, 121, 124, 125, 127, 171	Sanger, 'Lord' George	140, 163, 166
		Scalter-Booth, G MP	109, 116, 126
		Seventy Years a Showman	140
Manners, Lord John	70, 75, 76, 84	Shaftesbury, Lord	7–9, 45, 47, 59, 61, 66, 68–70, 75, 76, 138, 154, 175
Manning, Cardinal	152, 166		
Mayfield, Mary	31, 34	Shenstone, William	17
Melly, George, MP	71–3	Showmen	131, 136–40, 163
Menageries	136, 163	Sion College	170
Methodism	15, 17, 29, 30, 41, 44, 156	*Six Days in a Monkey Boat*	118
Methodism, Primitive	11, 14, 15, 17, 29, 30, 41–3, 52, 58, 67, 106, 156, 172	Smith, George	*passim*
		parentage and birth	Ch 1
Moira	102, 103	childhood, youth and marriage	Ch 2
Morley, John	103	at Ladderedge and Reapsmoor	Ch 3
Movable Dwellings Bill	152, 154, 161–3, 166, 170, 174	at Humberstone	Ch 3
		at Coalville	Ch 4
Munby, Arthur	137	campaigns for brick-yard children	Chs 5 & 6
Mundella, Anthony, MP	54, 58, 67, 68, 70, 71, 75, 76, 123, 151	campaigns for canal boat children	Chs 10–12
Museum, British	115, 158, 171	political work	Ch 8
Narrow Boats	96–8, 101	campaigns for 'travelling' children	Ch 13 & 14
Northend Brick and Tile Company	89, 90, 102		

INDEX

The Band of Love   Chs 15 & 16
     Death   172, 173
     'George Smith of Coalville Fund'
         128
Smith, John, (grandfather)   13
Smith, née Capper, Deborah,
     (grandmother)   10, 13
Smith, William, (father)   10–7, 42, 86, 87
Smith, née Hollins, Hannah,
     (mother)   13–6
Smith, née Mayfield, Mary,
     (1st wife)   31, 44, 51
Smith, née Lehman, Mary Ann,
     (2nd wife)   7, 51, 65, 75, 92, 119, 127, 171, 173, 174
Social Science Congresses: 59, 66, 153
     Newcastle   59, 63, 66, 72
     Plymouth   74, 76
     Liverpool   78, 108
     Manchester   143
     Edinburgh   118, 145
     Nottingham   147
     Huddersfield   124
Springfield House   39, 57, 58, 83
Staffordshire Sentinel   62
Stead, W.T.   128, 170
Stenson, William   37, 38
Stenson, William (son)   39
Stephens, H.C. MP   158, 160–3, 166
Stephenson, George   37, 38
Stephenson, Robert   37, 38
Sunday Schools   7, 30, 33, 34, 41, 43, 52, 59, 64, 76, 84, 86, 88

Temporary Dwellings Bill   159–61
Ten Hours Bill 1847   47
The Times   56, 57, 63, 94, 126
'Travelling' Children   Chs 13 & 14
Trent and Mersey Canal   14, 15, 87
Tunstall   14–7, 29–31, 34, 42, 62, 70, 85, 87, 96

UKSVDA   163, 164, 166–8

Victoria, Queen   8, 53, 54, 83, 87, 114, 142, 143, 149, 156
Walks in the Black Country   24
Wall Grange   32
Wedgwood, Betty Mrs.   17–20
Wedgwood, Josiah   15
Welton   119, 129, 167
Wemyss, Lord   161
Wesleyan Chapel   15, 16, 18, 34, 41
West, Harry   31, 32
Whetstone, James   39
White Cottage   156
Whitwick Colliery Company   35–9, 44, 46, 52, 57, 80, 81, 88, 89
Winter Journey   110–2, 117, 122
Workshops Act 1867   48, 49, 53, 56
Workshops Regulation Act 1871   48, 49